D0428845

STACKED

By the same author

Going with the Grain

STACKED

A 32DDD Reports
from the Front

Susan Seligson

BLOOMSBURY

Lyrics by Kayla Sosnow used by permission.

Published by Bloomsbury USA, New York
Distributed to the trade by Holtzbrinck Publishers

All papers used by Bloomsbury USA are natural,
recyclable products made from wood grown in well-managed
forests. The manufacturing processes conform to the
environmental regulations of the country of origin.

Library of Congress Cataloging-in-Publication Data

Seligson, Susan.
Stacked : a 32DDD reports from the front / Susan Seligson. — 1st U.S. ed.
p.   cm.
ISBN-13: 978-1-59691-117-8 (hardcover)
ISBN-10: 1-59691-117-4 (hardcover)
1. Breast—Social aspects.   2. Breast—Humor.   3. Body image in
women.   I. Title.

GT498.B74S45   2007
391.6—dc22
2006028137

First U.S. Edition 2007

1 3 5 7 9 10 8 6 4 2

Typeset by Westchester Book Group
Printed in the United States of America by Quebecor World Fairfield

In memory of my father, Isidor Seligson,
who adored women of all shapes and sizes

A man is dating three women and trying to decide which one to marry.

He gives each woman $5,000. The first goes to a salon for a complete makeover and spends the rest on jewelry and clothes. The second buys the man fancy gifts like computers, golf clubs, and a watch. The third girlfriend invests the $5,000 in the stock market, earns several times that amount, gives the man back his $5,000, and reinvests the rest.

Which woman does he marry?

The one with the biggest tits.

*   *   *

. . . the old janitor on his deathbed
Who demands to see the breasts of his wife
For the one last time
Is the greatest poet who ever lived.

—Charles Simic, "Breasts"

CONTENTS

Introduction:
My Face Is Up Here, Pal

O NE SPRING DAY in Central Park I crossed paths with a generously endowed woman wearing a T-shirt with an arrow and the words "My face is up here, pal." I longed to give her a sisterly hug. I restrained myself not only because we were strangers to each other, but also because I feared the mayhem that might result from such a collision of boobs. Still I looked her right in her lovely, underappreciated eyes and offered a nod of solidarity. All too often my own face plays a supporting role to the main attraction, my 32DDD breasts.

That is not a typo. Allow me to help you with the math. Proportionally speaking, this is the equivalent of the USS *Nimitz* anchored in a pond. My bra size makes me, in the eyes of Maidenform at least, a freak. In the days before rampant breast augmentation, the juxtaposition of such immense breasts with such a diminutive frame confounded bra manufacturers. Elsie, saleswoman emerita at the downtown Boston Filene's, referred to me as "her 32DDD." She'd special-order one Lilyette minimizer for me, and another for a customer from Newton, a nameless sister-in-stackdom for whom I'd developed an irrational affection. Elsie did the best she could. But these bras had the sex appeal of a truss. With very few exceptions, the men in my life have felt compelled at one time or another to wear one of these bras on their heads. Ha, ha, ha. As a kid at summer camp I had a counselor with outsized breasts, whom my bunkmates and I taunted by imprisoning a live toad in the tentlike cups of her bra. All these years later, in a karmic twist this woman would no doubt find hilarious, I don brassieres that could hold a viable terrarium.

I can't recall ever having small breasts. I remember having no breasts, but it seems I went from the Great Plains to the Tetons in the blink of an eye. I was two years ahead of myself in public school, and so the very last of my classmates to develop. While the bodies of my friends sprouted breasts, curves, and pubic hair, mine remained pudgy and babyish. I didn't begin menstruating until ninth grade. I was twelve years old at the time and existing in a state of unrelenting embarrassment and mortification. The boys I liked had five o'clock shadows. To them I was a freckled android in pigtails. We were great pals, but the only time boys wanted to get really close to me was during a geometry test. "Well," says my mother, "you certainly showed them." By the time I started college, at age sixteen, the rest of me finally stopped growing, but my breasts didn't quit. I still remember the day, in my late teens, when my mother studied me as I climbed out of the tub and declared, "You overreacted."

There are mornings, in the days just before my period, when my breasts are so heavy I find myself carrying them as I walk to the bathroom. They are fleshy torpedoes, exploding from my narrow shoulders, hovering ominously above my tiny waist. They're pale, warm, and smooth. They can conceal not one, but an entire pack of pencils. They can be cradled like puppies or made to slap each other like window weights. They're ridiculous.

It is within this Stupefyin' Jones body that I must greet the world. It's not that the rest of me is particularly hard on the eyes. But there are times I'm convinced that my breasts would attract a comparable level of admiration if they were to amble along the street on their own. During the years we spent summers in Woodstock, New York, there was a local fellow who liked to dog me as I strolled downtown, his attention wholly consumed by my breasts as they presented themselves under a T-shirt, tank top, or summer frock. This became an everyday occurrence. The man was harmless but irritating as hell. Only his status in the town's sixties hall of fame—his frontal lobe having succumbed to a variety of potent hallucinogens long ago—prevented me from seeking a restraining order. When I return for visits in the dead of winter, wrapped in fleecy layers, I sometimes find myself face-to-face with this same man. He registers not the faintest spark of recognition as he makes his way along Tinker Street. Breasts obscured, I may as well consist of vapor. Similar scenarios have played themselves out so many times in my life, I've come to believe that I can significantly alter the events of my day by either flaunting my breasts or hiding them. I'm Pussy Galore, or I'm Yentl.

What is it about an anatomical feature possessed by half of humanity that can render the other half senseless? No other body part looms so large in the human imagination. While there are around a hundred slang words for penis, there are many hundreds for breasts. There is such a profusion of big-breast websites—millions of hits last I checked, and that's just for *big* ones—that scores of them serve as mere gateways to the others. If you're a busy guy, bigbooblinks.com can propel you to boobywood.com before you can say Tawny Peaks. Pour

yourself a tequila and visit titfiesta.com. For you intergalactic
types, beam yourself to boobplanet.com. Prefer amateurs? Check
out Ilovemycleavage.com. Into full disclosure? Let me direct you
to yesthey'refake.com.

Who was it that said, "If you've seen two, you've seen 'em
all?" What would he make of the ever-expanding recession-
proof industry that spawned *Juggs* and *Busty Beauties* magazines? You'd think that, with this embarrassment of boob-riches
at their fingertips, men would grow weary of this writer's unair-
brushed pair, prosaic by comparison.

At age fifty-one, I sometimes take a detached, almost academic interest in the way my bust-to-waist-to-hips ratio continues to jangle the brains of teenaged stock clerks and of the
pensioners in golf shorts who shuffle along the aisles of the
kosher grocery near my mother's condo. And I have welcomed
the tenderness and reverence my breasts have inspired over the
years in the men I've loved. But at times I wish I owned an
emergency burka. It could be tightly folded into a snug packet,
like a space blanket, and I could reach into my purse and be
completely enshrouded within seconds. I remember meeting a
cross-dresser whose linebacker frame was crammed into a
vinyl miniskirt and tight sweater, prosthetic titties thrusting
forth like twin Matterhorns. "If I had a body like yours," he
said, "I'd dress like this all the time." "The hell you would," I
sweetly replied.

What doors, if any, have opened for me because of my large
breasts? Do I have them to thank for the mechanic who said
"No charge today," for the airport screener who volunteered
cheerfully to mail my contraband pocketknife to me, or for the
cop who insisted on providing an escort to an address in a
strange city? How many situations in my life might have played
out differently had I chosen to wear a different shirt that day?

One historical account tells of the fourth-century B.C. prostitute Phryne who was spared the death penalty after baring her breasts to the judges. It's a testament to enduring breast lust that this story survives the long, populous march of history, along with the wardrobe functions and malfunctions of Dolly Parton and Janet Jackson.

How many millions of men could have written, in all honesty, the following personal from the *London Review of Books*: "I like you because you read magazines with big words. And you've got great booblies. I can live without the first. But the second is non-negotiable. Shallow man, 34 . . ."

It isn't just men; everyone's obsessed with breasts. Toddlers are enthralled with my "boobies," my women friends marvel at them, my doctor and I puzzle over how much they weigh. Even the poker-faced mammographer is not above a good-natured wisecrack or two. The most lugubrious one will smile when the machine begins rolling south with my boob still in it. "Excuse me," I say. "Those are attached." My 32DDDs also captivate my gay male friends, who display an abiding curiosity about their erotic sensitivity.

Apparently this fascination isn't even limited to members of my own species. Once when I went to give a pat to my friend Heidi's two-hundred-pound goat, the beast gummed my right breast so passionately it left a bruise. I was reminded of this when I read recently of a lawsuit filed against the Gorilla Foundation by two women who maintained that Koko, the "talking" gorilla, was breast-obsessed. In the course of the women's sessions with her, Koko was insistent in her sign language requests for them to show her their nipples.

I'll give Koko the benefit of the doubt and decide that her curiosity is less prurient than scientific. After all, when it comes to our breasts, human females are alone in the animal kingdom.

Other mammals grow plump breasts only when pregnant or lactating. But a set of DDD knockers can bring out the ape in anyone. Here are just a few of the less idyllic encounters that can befall a woman of my gifts.

I set out on Truro's Longnook Beach one balmy fall morning for a long walk with my twin mutts, Manny and Fanny. Just one other car was parked in the lot. At the bottom of the dune I encountered a lone fisherman. We exchanged greetings and small talk about the weather. A while later, when I returned to my car, the fisherman was gone but I saw, written in the veil of dirt on the rear windshield, the words NICE TITS.

When I was just seventeen, a friend and I spent a summer touring Europe on the cheap. Joining the sweaty crowd at the Louvre, we waited our turn to gape at the *Mona Lisa*. Just when I came face-to-face with that cryptic smile, a man's arm emerged seemingly from nowhere to tweak my left nipple really hard. Just as swiftly the arm receded; I never saw his face. On a recent solo trip to Rome, I flagged a taxi to take me across the river to Trastevere. I chatted with the driver in my kiddy Italian. When we reached my destination I thanked him warmly and handed him the fare plus a generous tip. In one continuous motion, he pocketed the cash and grabbed my breast.

On rare occasions, the tit man on the street has been surprisingly polite, even genteel. "Pardon me, miss," said an expensively suited businessman as he strode toward me on a crowded avenue in Hempstead, New York. "But you really have beautiful breasts. I'd like to get a look at them, if I may. I'd pay you ten dollars and I promise I won't lay a hand on you." I was all of eighteen. I pushed my way past this weirdo, but to this day regret not asking, "Ten dollars for each, or the pair?"

Living life, as the personals would put it, as a BBW has made me concerned for my safety. I'm not talking about the risk of getting my nipples caught in an elevator door, though I'm sure it's possible. I'm talking about walking home at night on a near deserted street when my breasts might make me appear juicier than the usual prey. But it was in benign daylight, when my guard was down, that my breasts put me in the most imminent danger. Dressed in a tank top and shorts and out walking my dog one infernally hot summer afternoon in Boston, I was on a stately stretch of Commonwealth Avenue when I noticed a man cruising alongside me in his car, matching my pace and looking at my breasts as if they belonged to him but had been stolen years ago. "Nice tits," he called, craning his head out the window in my direction. Seconds later he plowed into a lamppost. He got out of the car to survey the damage, which was considerable, and cursed me as I beat a retreat to my apartment.

In retrospect, some of my breast-related experiences might have been actionable. For example, there was my boss at a weekly newspaper who prefaced a demanding assignment with the words, "I didn't just hire you because you have great tits, you know." But over the years I have served up justice in my own way. In graduate school I worked at a high-toned consulting firm where one of the pedigreed Harvard graduates had a habit of addressing work-related comments directly to my breasts. One day, in a fit of exasperation, I grabbed my right breast and gave it a chirpy falsetto as I moved it up and down in reply. Once on a muggy day at a summer office job, my grandfatherly boss asked to "have a word." "You do a good job," he said. "And you're fortunate to be a well-endowed young woman. But I'm going to have to ask you to wear loose blouses when you come to work here. My salesmen are having trouble concentrating."

I needed the job. But I followed my instincts, and my boobs and I got the hell out of there. I wasn't the most articulate or motivated feminist at the time but I still knew the problem was his, not mine. He called for days, and sent flowers, but I never went back. It was decades later, after back surgery and countless cries of "Nice tits!" in a string of languages, that I considered making the problem go away by the only means available to me. I would go under the knife and cash those DDDs in for a saner set of Cs, maybe even Bs. That was when I met Nancy. Nancy had a tight, boyish runner's body. She had closely cropped hair and wore halters and short shorts. She reminded me of Peter Pan. One day she whispered to me, "You know, my breasts used to be as big as yours."

The revelation stunned me. I'd always considered myself as belonging to a different species from women who look like Nancy. Like many women who are thrilled with the results of their breast reductions, Nancy insisted the surgery could change my life. I took her up on her offer to show me her compact new breasts. Without examining them too closely, I detected two inverted T-shaped scars. And though I could be wrong, it seemed to me that the nipples pointed at odd angles, like airplane reading lights in need of adjustment.

"Aren't they fabulous?" she asked.

Though I couldn't quite agree, I did allow myself to fantasize about unhooking and hooking my bra without an ensuing gravitational thud. Imagine crossing over to that other species, for which loose straps *don't* mean flabby tits. How lovely to see a bra as a sexy wisp of a thing, not an over-the-shoulder-boulderholder. Consider an existence in which certain yoga poses don't carry the risk of suffocation by one's own bosom.

Sure, it would be great not to have to hear another saleswoman tell me a sports bra is "one size fits . . . um . . . I can't help you, honey." But I've endured surgery of the nonbreast variety several times. It's awful. Instead of taking that journey I've decided to embark on a different one. I have chosen to lay breast obsession bare—to enter, as it were, the belly of the boob.

In the pages that follow, for less than, oh, the price of two pickets to Titsburgh, I will take you to the heart of breast culture. The tour is not for the squeamish. Tag along with my boobs and me as we step into scrubs and enter the sterile confines of the operating room where tender flesh is sliced and sculpted. Join us as we linger in the raucous lair of the exotic dancer and wend our way from the academic perch of the anthropologist to the dressing rooms of the legendary retail institution that lives by the boast "No bra size too bizarre." Allow me to be your guide from the battle lines of the topfreedom crusade to the editorial offices of *Busty Beauties*. Browse alongside me in an ever-burgeoning marketplace of vacuum-powered breast developers, water-padded corsets, "bust-enhancing" creams, pills, patches, and chewing gum. Travel with me through time over centuries of lifting, separating, binding, wrapping, squashing, exposing, enshrouding, scaffolding, and piercing.

In the course of writing this book I have seesawed between two mind-sets. Breasts no big deal; breasts very big deal. I go back and forth not just on the subject of breasts in general but in contemplating my own twins, girls, gazungas, palookas, whatever. I never cease to be stunned by what's lurking out there in cyberspace: freebigtits, brababes, verylargebreasts, bigperkybreasts, boobieindex, boobsource, time4tits, onlybreasts, and on and on and on. What are these people, five years old? And yet among the straight men I know there is not one, no matter how polished, tweedy, intellectual, fusty, or geriatric, who doesn't go instantly stupid when I divulge the subject of my book. I may slip into high-minded mode with clinical phrases like "breast obsession" or "breast fetishism." I may share my interest in breast evolution or breast fixation across cultures. The men listen patiently, and then ask: Will there be pictures?

Among women, meanwhile, boobs are also a subject of endless fascination. It didn't really matter where I was, when I mentioned the topic of this book the women around me, friends and strangers, poured out their stories, observations, and complaints. I was discussing the book with Kate, my hairdresser, when we realized the rest of the salon had fallen silent. Finally the receptionist piped up with a boob story, joined by the other women in the room. At a friend's fiftieth-birthday party where I knew no one except my friend's husband and kids, I struck up a conversation with a woman that led to my revealing the subject of my book. We were off and running. "Boobs!" she cried. "I have boobs! Yes I do! I'm sick of hiding them under floppy shirts!" When she heard about the book, my best friend's young daughter offered herself as an interview subject. She'd just graduated from a women's college in Los Angeles. "We talked boobs all the time," she told me. "My friends and I are completely obsessed with boobs." A woman I met on the trail where I walk my dogs stopped me to say she'd heard about my project and asked if I would like to hear about her boobs. "They're gigantic," she said, "and they've had a life of their own."

At the start of my research I requested a Google "Alert" every time the word "breast" surfaced on any online news website. By the next day the alerts were rolling in, and there hasn't been a day since without one or more, each containing at least three references. Only a few of these a week were chicken recipes.

From around the globe, the dispatches flowed. There were stories, far too many to cite in full, of various authority figures succumbing to breast lust on the job. In New Haven a pulmonary specialist massaged and kissed a patient's breasts, also complimenting them as "soft and beautiful," during an examination. The woman had complained of a sinus infection. During private singing lessons, a Los Angeles music teacher touched his teenaged pupils' breasts while pretending to show them the location of their diaphragms. In Lincolnshire, England, a general practitioner told a patient complaining of stomach pain to lift up her bra. He proceeded to cup and bounce her breasts and told her that her "big bosoms" were the cause of her problems. She filed a complaint and visited another doctor, who diagnosed gallstones. A neurologist in Wales was charged with fondling the breasts of an epileptic patient.

Though I rarely encountered any meaningful cyber chat about breasts, I stumbled on a guide to online shorthand for boobs. For example, these are perfect breasts: (0)(0). Breasts augmented with implants are (+)(+), while high-nippled breasts are (@)(@). Lopsided breasts are, logically, (o)(0); pierced breasts are (Q)(Q); A-cup breasts are oo; and your grandma's breasts are \o/\o/. In my cyber travels I also located what I believe to be the least visited site on the Internet: flatchestedbabes.com.

Having lugged this pair around all these years, I assumed I knew quite a bit about breasts. I was wrong. My teachers included Dr. Roger Khouri, an esteemed plastic surgeon and tissue regeneration expert who invented the Brava breast enhancement system in the hope of both sparing women the scalpel and profiting from their mass fixation on what he calls "two stupid mounds of flesh." I will share what I learned in the gentle, sage company of the renowned surgeon and essayist Robert Goldwyn, a professor emeritus at Harvard Medical School. You will grow acquainted with Guinness World Record holder Maxi Mounds, whose exotic dancing and porn careers swelled along with breasts surgically enhanced until they hit the off-the-charts size of beach balls. My self-styled boob tour led me to the perky charms and Beverly Hills boob factory of the buff, mischievous Robert Rey, aka "Dr. 90210," he of the tight black surgical scrubs.

It seems ridiculous that one even has to say that there is much more to being a woman than having breasts. Yet in Western culture, and increasingly around the world—China, for example, recently outlawed a dangerous and disfiguring "man-made fat" named Ao Mei Ding after nearly 300,000 women had paid to have it injected into their breasts—breasts are an essential marker of womanhood. For better or worse, they are the shorthand for, and the badge of, femininity. I've met formerly small-breasted women who resorted to getting implants because they didn't "feel like women." Society pelts us at every turn with the message that the bigger our breasts, the more of a woman we are. While some women undergo surgery to achieve cartoonishly outsized boobs, women like me are frustrated and wearied by being reduced to a walking pair of tits. Among the amply endowed, breast reduction surgery beckons as the antidote to the catcall as well as the backache.

What I heard from women friends and acquaintances reinforced what every woman intuitively knows—that from their first chaste appearance onward, breasts are by far the most emotionally fraught and irksome of body parts. We have plenty of reasons to cherish our breasts. They give us and our partners great sexual pleasure into old age. Most miraculous of all, they are often the sole sustenance of our babies, whom we hold to our breasts in the species' most primal and enduring expression of unconditional love.

In the pages that follow I will explore what breasts mean to their bearers as well as their beholders, and what happens when we see womanhood reflected in these mysterious, oddly powerful body parts.

As he poked away at the breast tissue of a patient about to receive saline implants, a cosmetic surgeon remarked to me that women with big breasts are more successful in love, and life in general. "Let's face it," he said, busying himself with something that resembled a lug wrench, "they just do better in life."

Hmm. Well, this indisputable fact would certainly explain my own copious wealth, far-reaching professional success, and otherwise charmed existence. Do people truly believe this? Is life markedly different for the triple-Ds of the world? And if so, how, and why?

Somewhat fearful of what I might learn, I set out to find the answer.

Nice Chi-chis

WHEN I BEGAN my search for breast slang, without which no tit, I mean knocker, I mean boob book would be complete, I soon realized I was facing a task that could easily balloon out of control. At the start I wondered whether this pursuit was even worthy of the word "research," considering that over the years many of these terms have been hurled, gratis, in my direction. Forget the etymologists and lexicographers; if I want synonyms for breasts, I need only venture out in public.

A boob man could manage in this world equipped with only this short list: tits, jugs, knockers, hooters, and rack, an inexplicable favorite of one of my lesbian friends. But these are the tip of the iceboo— I mean, iceberg. If you want to talk boobs, there are hundreds, perhaps thousands, of terms on a list that is expanding even as I write.

Breast terms defy normal linguistic strictures. Most words for common things enter our language by traceable means: either because they're descriptive ("rod" for penis), borrowed from other languages ("thug," from the Hindi *thugee*; "assassin" from the hash-smoking, homicidal *hashishin* of Arabic), ono-matopoetic ("achoo!"), paying tribute ("half-Nelson," "pasteurize"), or from a subcultural patois gone mainstream ("Chill," "dis"). And certainly many terms for breasts have origins that fit these categories. But, as the tireless word collector Richard Spears points out to me, you can coin breast terms from absolutely anything, even gibberish. The only requirement is that the word be plural.

"There's the numbers game," says Spears, the author of several lexicons including *Slang and Euphemism,* who confesses that breast words try his patience as a linguist. These terms are inspired by everything and anything. Much of what anyone concludes about them fails to rise above speculation. The situation is simply out of hand. When it comes to anatomical slang, Spears says, "if you name a word that you don't understand in the singular, it's probably a penis. In the plural it's breasts. If you talk about bazongies, 95 percent of people will guess breasts. Any mysterious references to female anatomy in the plural will be assumed to be breasts."

So, presumably, a guy can have a big bazongo while his girlfriend has big bazongies. Spears and I happen to have just made these up, but they say it all. Breast slang has a lot in common with family slang. There are as many ways to say "poop" as we can imagine, and more. Some of these words seep into the mainstream, and some wither and die at the address where they were born.

We have hooters; why not pookalookas? I think I just made that one up, too, but maybe not. We have headlights, melons, coconuts, and jugs. Why not Nerf balls, or rutabagas? Name your own, name a friend's, name everyone's. Proper names are accepted, even embraced. Now get your slimy paws off my Kathie Lee Giffords.

"Some breast words have really good and obvious explanations," observes Spears. "There's norks, for example. There's an Australian dairy company called Norco and their advertisements show pictures of cows' udders." But if there's a clear parallel, says Spears, "anything the size of a lemon or larger can be breasts." And, no matter how descriptively off-base the word is, when it comes to breast slang, there's no ambiguity. For example, if I were strolling along the street in a tight knit top and a construction worker called out "Nice cowabungas!" from his scaffolded perch, would there be any doubt he's referring to my boobs? Men admire and are often smitten by legs, eyes, or buttocks. But it's boobs that inspire a breakthrough level of creativity.

Spears points out that as the prevailing breast term, "boobs" is the most innocuous and the only one that has gained widespread acceptance. That's because it's the slang term women are most likely to use in reference to their own breasts. A woman might complain how her boobs ache, sag, or feel lumpy. But I strongly doubt anyone has ever shared concerns with a girlfriend about discomfort in her hooters. And I'd be surprised to learn that somewhere some woman is confiding to her mammographer that she feels a thickening in her right knocker.

I've always felt comfortable saying "boobs" in nearly all types of company. My stepgranddaughter has always extolled the virtues of my "boobies." Who could possibly be offended by the word "boobs"? Absolutely no one, I'd assumed. But I was wrong about this. My husband and I were at a fancy dinner thrown by the publisher of the weekly newspaper in which my column appears, in honor of the paper's tenth anniversary. There was no assigned seating, so our table shaped up to be a haphazard collection of people from graphics, editorial, accounting, and the front desk. When the conversation found its way to my latest project, everyone at the table was eager to talk boobs, except for a lone receptionist. She stared down at her plate, looking embarrassed and a little ill. Her friend suddenly gasped and said, "Oh, I forgot. She hates that word." " 'Boobs?' " we all chimed in. By now the woman was practically in tears. She didn't just dislike the word "boobs," she appeared to be allergic to it. "Could you please *stop*?" she whimpered. If we would not, she said, she'd have to leave.

Of course we were then off and running about words we, as women, hate. Most despised: "cunt," although a few women thought the word had been reinvented and de-sullied by Eve Ensler's *Vagina Monologues*. None of us liked "tits." Also: "bitch," though this wasn't unanimous. But "boobs"? For one thing, "boobs" and "boobies" are words beloved by children, which in my mind makes them as innocuous as "doody."

Of course, maybe that's just me. A lot of these feelings stem from a woman's upbringing. In my parents' house no one had a problem with the word "shit." "Fuck" was excused as an exclamation and "fucking" was forgiven as an adjective only. "Fuck" the verb was pretty much off-limits. "Fuck you!" got past the censors only when directed at a politician on the TV screen, or inanimate objects such as the rusty nail that just pierced one's bare foot. The worst thing a kid could say in our house was "Shut up." That alone could get you grounded. As for "cunt," it was so taboo that to utter the word would have been the equivalent of spreading mayonnaise on a lamb chop. "Schmuck" was permissible, while the synonymous "prick" was not. But people are different. My friends were amazed by my parents' laissez-faire attitude toward "shit." I'm sure my mother would've recoiled had I referred to my boobs as "tits."

She would have found that vulgar. Yet I have friends who grew up referring, without a shred of shame, to their "titties."

"Don't forget there's a very strong class element in this," Spears says. "On the low end of the scale you find 'tits,' 'jugs.' Traveling around the country these last few years, I've learned that poor people talk different than rich people." Spears talks about words in flux, how an event can open the door for a taboo word to become mainstream. He offers the example of the way the *Vagina Monologues* might lift inhibitions on the word "vagina." "But if they used *The Pussy Monologues*, well, that's a real taboo in the language."

Though many breast terms are downright crude, many are refreshingly ironic. A few are nothing less than poetic. Some live on in their original context, like *Ulysses'* Leopold Bloom pondering the "heaving embonpoint" in *Sweets of Sin,* or in Woody Allen's "May I cop a feel off thy royal tomatoes?"

I mined the synonym dictionaries and online lists for compelling and inscrutable foreign terms. If I were to amble along the streets of Cologne, for example, would the driver of a passing BMW remark on the heft of my farfegneugens? Might a rudely unrestrained Oaxacan try to grope my chalupas? It helps to know that if someone in Tokyo politely asks to see your chiku-bis, he is referring to your nipples. A Romanian might be momentarily transfixed by my balconi. Was it the Mormons who, in a fit of ancestral pride, coined the term "Salt Lake Cities"? My friend Duane informs me that the London blokes prefer "mammaries" to "tits," though they also might call attention to a flat-chested woman's "fried eggs." Flat-chested women tend to wince at the words "mosquito bites." But hopefully they'd get a giggle out of "pirate's dream." As in, sunken chest. Is there such an oxymoronic thing, I wonder, as a "flat-chested broad"?

To get a better grip, so to speak, on the vast variety of breast terms, I grouped them into general categories. Here is a selection:

The crude: pimples, breastasauri, top bollocks, cat heads, cock warmers, dugs, feedbags, flesh fillets, jelly bells, man puppets, nipple caddies, paw patties, rib flaps, shirt potatoes, warts, whammers, lung nuts, all-day suckers, chesticles, and, rather disgustingly, chest hams. Even more disgusting is a term I uncovered for nipples: clam necks.

There are terms paying geographical homage. And they are all over the map. Consider: Boston wobblers, Bristol cities, Caracas, capitol domes, Dutch Alps, the Gland Canyon, hemispheres, Grand Tetons, Jersey Cities, Kanchenjungas, Minneapolis and St. Paul, Pyramids, Rangoons, Fujiyamas, Tahitis, Tora Boras, Babylons, Eigers, Idahos.

I also came upon an abundance of breast terms honoring the famous and the infamous, both individuals and teams. Some are glaringly obvious, like Dolly Partons or, and this I find adorable, the Pointer Sisters. Others are confounding and a little creepy—why Eric and Lyle? Is somebody somewhere diddling the nipples of his lover's Leopold and Loebs?

Here is a sampling: Abbott and Costello, Ben and Jerry, Bert and Ernie, Bob and Ray, Brad Pitts, Eartha Kitts, Bonnie and Clyde, Danny DeVitos, David and Goliath, Eisenhowers, Lewinskis, Durantes, Godzillas, Fred and Ethel, Holmes and Watson, Isaac Newtons, John and Paul, Mahatmas, Mobutus, Mickey and Minnie, Mike and Ike, Pia Zadoras, Murphys, Mulligans, Thelma and Louise, Tweedledee and Tweedledum, Wilsons, George and Gracie, Lilo and Stitch.

To these I might add my own Bella and Sadie. (Now you know.) And who knows how many others thrive in far-flung pockets of the world. Is there, for example, somewhere in

Calcutta a generously endowed Bengali woman massaging coconut oil into her Mukherjees?

Because, as Spears points out, most breast terms are coined
by men, it makes sad sense that there would be a plethora of
breast terms drawn from the military lexicon. I found scores
of these, including cannonballs, cruise missiles, thirty-eights,
warheads, dirigibles, guns, doughboys, El Primo torpedos,
gunboats, helicopters, ICBMs, howitzers, bombshells, lethal
weapons, lacto grenades, Mausers, nukes, pontoons, launch
codes, radar domes, satellites, Sherman tanks, Smith & Wes-
son, stun grenades, minesweepers, TNTs, U-boats, zeppelins,
and my very favorite, shock and awe.

What makes far more sense to me, as a female, is the inclina-
tion to name breasts for fruits, vegetables, and ethnic delicacies.
Like coconuts, cantaloupes, pumpkins, and torta, breasts are
tantalizing and yummy. A guy could be forgiven, or perhaps even
rewarded, for taking note of his lover's tortellinis. But it's the
Mexican menu that makes the largest contribution. No mystery
there when you read from the list: casabas, carumbas, chalupas,
chi-chis, chimichangas, concitas, enchiladas, garbanzos, mam-
marambas, margaritas, mangos, tamales, and tortillas.

To me, the most annoying category draws its inspiration
from an inescapable, testosterone-infused trapping of modern
society—the automobile. Fondle my chimichangas, tweak my
Tetons, diddle my Dolly Partons. But please, guys, don't heap
praise on my distributor caps. Ditto my airbags, *amortisseurs*
(French for "shock absorbers"), bumpers, Goodyears, grill-
work, headlights, high beams, hood ornaments, honkers, hub-
caps, rivets, rotors, rib bumpers, blinkers, Volvos, snow tires,
speed bumps, windshield wipers, or Winnebagos.

For car-inspired breast metaphors gone awry, I quote Dan
McKay of Fargo, North Dakota, the 2005 winner of the

Bulwer-Lytton Fiction Contest for the worst opening sentence. "As he stared at her ample bosom, he daydreamed of the dual Stromberg carburetors in his vintage Triumph Spitfire, highly functional yet pleasingly formed, perched prominently on top of the intake manifold, aching for experienced hands, the small knurled caps of the oil dampeners begging to be inspected and adjusted as described in chapter seven of the shop manual."

Among the terms in Wikipedia, the most exhaustive list I could find, are a few—just a smattering—that strike me as purely sweet and touching. What woman wouldn't melt at her partner's tribute to her love muffins? There are even expressions fueled by religious fervor. Let me gaze upon your minarets. Let me worship at your altars. Let me hang my cap on your chapel hat pegs. Okay, maybe that last one doesn't quite do it. But I am charmed by the tenderness and wit of the following: Claire de Lunes, doppelgängers, golden domes, home sweet home, parabolas, oblations, pride and joy, au bord bainne, avant-postes. There is also "loaves of love," which sounds more like a charity soup kitchen, and "quantum heaps," no doubt coined by a horny particle physicist, which, in my experience, is a redundancy. You'd think there would be more musical terms, but the few I found captured my fancy. One can only hope the late Vladimir Horowitz consoled himself by burying his sad face in his wife's Moonlight Sonatas.

As for terms that are nonsensical yet somehow hit the nail on the head, the possibilities, as I mentioned earlier, are endless. Some that have already worked their way into the boob lexicon: babaloos, baloobas, bazoombas, bijongas, billibongs, boops, cha-chas, chumbawumbas, dinglebobbers, flapdoodles, gazongas, gobstoppers, goombas, jahoobies, kagemushas, kawangas, mau maus, nay-nays, neeners, num-nums, palookas, pushmatahas, shabba-dos, shlobes, shmozobs, soombas, spla-zoingas, tatas, teetees, tishomingos, twekkers, wahwahs, whim-whams, wopbopaloobops, yazoos, ying-yangs.

I find many of these inspired. I really don't think I'd be pissed off if a strange man enthused over my shmozobs. Call me twisted, but I might even want to get to know this guy.

And finally, there are those who feel compelled to name breasts for their original and too often forgotten purpose. Wikipedia offers these, to cite a few: baby feeders, bottles, dairy pillows, God's milk bottles, milk bombs, milkshakes, milk wagons, milk jugs. I hate these. I'm not sure why, but they annoy me as much as if someone decided to call a penis a sperm spigot or . . . I'll stop there.

Though otherwise profoundly unappealing to me, a career as an exotic dancer or porn actress holds one small attraction. I would have a great time trying to come up with a stage name. Few of these women use their real name or anything close. This is, after all, an industry in which working agents go by first names only. I have a collection of business cards that say, for example, "Wide World Entertainment. Bruce." Culling websites like photoclubs.com's Ultimate Big Boob Collection I found the best examples of breast slang enlisted for creative stage names. Dee Dee Deluxxx, Kimberly Kupps, Pandora Peaks, Honey Melons, and of course, my gal pals Maxi Mounds, Crystal Gunns, and Kayla Kupcakes. There's Chesty Malone and Busty Dusty, Tiffany Towers and Melody Foxxxe. There's Lana Lotts, Busty Bozena, Jugged Desirae, Alexis Amore, and Daphne . . . *Rosen*??? There it is, surrounded by the Brandies, Busties, and Tiffanys of titspost.com: "Voluptuous Boobed Daphne Rosen."

Hmm. Perhaps I wouldn't need a stage name after all. I could be myself, just like Daphne Rosen is herself. And if there are guys who can't deal with that, well, they don't get to see my latkes.

Our Boobs, Ourselves

M Y EARLIEST MEMORY of my maternal grandmother is the feel and scent of her cleavage. Her skin was papery and freckled from too much sun, and her cleavage was, or seemed to me at the time, vast, cavernous, and capable of cradling my entire face. She stashed things in there. A handkerchief. Cash. Her reading glasses. Like most Jewish grand matrons of her generation, she smelled like soap and potted meat. Her bras were unlike those of my mother. Grandma's brassieres, as she called them, were prosaic and clinical looking and hung stiff on the shower door, the cups two skullcaps of heavy cotton. The bras' utilitarian drabness was a surprising counterpoint to my grandmother's elegant, feminine wardrobe. She loved being stylish and remained a clotheshorse until her death at ninety-two. As she aged, her hair fell out, she wore dentures, and she lost a breast to a mastectomy. When she visited she shared my room and I recall being far more horrified by seeing her wigless than by her mastectomy scars.

Boobs were big in my family, in every way. On my mother's side was a lineup of zaftig women who as they aged developed the kind of breasts that, imprisoned in scary eight-hook bras, formed an immense sloping shelf. Released from their under-garments, my great-aunts' breasts were not only pendulous but also projected in opposite directions. There was the eastward boob and the westward boob, and never the twain did meet. Not even close. You could play soccer on the flesh that stretched between them. I don't know how these women managed to keep their bodies upright. The aunts would home in on one of us kids at a family funeral or bar mitzvah, their menacing water-balloon breasts hovering just above their midsections. I'd hesitate to call that part of their bodies a waist. A waist was something no woman among my relations could claim. A waist was an attribute possessed by film stars and gentiles.

Boobs took on a special weight, so to speak, at the seashore. I can still see them all: Fanny, Tessie, Bertha, and Grandma Julia plotzed along the tide line like so many walruses. When I was very small I thought this was what people meant by "swimming"—the scooping of chilly water into one's bosom while exclaiming "Oooh! Aaah! Oy!" For this, they wore bathing suits resembling flowered beer barrels, and bathing caps, elaborate ones ranging in design from tufted daisies to acrylic fright wigs. Thanks to this bunch, and also to a good number of the postchildbearing matrons and grand matrons gathered with their families nearby, the beach was like a perpetual contest of who could look the least appealing. This, to me, was the defini-tion of being old: you stopped making yourself cute for the beach and began dressing in a beer barrel and a fright wig, with zinc oxide ointment coating your nose for good measure.

I will never stop being cute, I vowed to myself. I will never wear a bathing suit that retains my shape when I'm not in it. I will never wear a bathing cap of any kind. And I will never have boobs that are intimately acquainted with my belly button.

And here I am now, my bare breasts just itching to give my belly button a kiss. I have made peace with my breasts, but so many women I know are at war with theirs. Even among those who like their breasts, I have known few women, young or old, to claim outright infatuation with their boobs. (Women who've had implants or artfully done breast reductions are an exception.) How nice it would be if we could all sing their praises, in the manner of this entry in the "best of" section of craigslist.org: "Boobs are just FUN. It's like a stress ball that's always with you, a dangling slinky attached to your body. It is a continuous source of beautiful, bouncy amusement. . . . My boobies have vim and vigor! They are ready to go in the morning!"

Vim and vigor? Who is this crackpot? Most large-breasted women I know complain that after a long day of imprisonment their boobs are tender and dejected. And at least among their owners, the ripe and, oh, all right, vigorous breasts of teenagers and young women are not habitually given the appreciation they're due. For teenaged girls especially, as Dr. Kristen Harrison, media researcher at the University of Illinois, puts it, life is "one opportunity after another to feel lousy about yourself." No pubescent girl with big breasts is happy about them. It takes years for a young woman, if she's lucky, to embrace and grow to like them. Even the ubiquitous nymphet Jessica Simpson confessed that, as a young girl, she was self-conscious and "made to feel guilty" about her precocious breasts. "And now," she observes, "people are buying the boobs I have!"

Presumably, any woman with a sex life is accustomed to having her breasts kissed, fondled, even worshipped. I have never been with a man who said, "Your breasts are okay but I'd like them a lot better if they were firmer and perkier." In fact, I've never been with a man who didn't adore them just the way they are. What kind of dolt, when served up with a woman's bare breasts, would dare to find fault with them? For all their fixation on the Pamela Andersons of the world, most men are satisfied with what they've been handed. And even as we yield gratefully to the erotic pleasure afforded by breasts of any size, many of us react as we would if someone were to compliment our outfit: "What . . . these old things?"

To be sure, there are women who are quietly enamored of their breasts. She writes no paeans to their vim and vigor, but a thirty-four-year-old woman I know thinks her 34C breasts are "the perfect handful." Though she is forever finding fault with the rest of her body, at least in the boob department, Ariel says, "I got lucky. They're not veiny or hairy, the areola size is just like a bottle cap—just the right size. They're real pretty, and perky, though they've certainly dropped over the years." Stealing a comparative glance at other naked women in the locker room, Ariel will spy the legs she longs for, or an enviable ass. "But," she adds, "if I look at someone else's breasts, I think mine are nicer."

Ariel's affection for her breasts is heartening. But to judge by the ever escalating mania to enhance or otherwise modify healthy, perfectly serviceable breasts, she is a refreshing exception. And as satisfied as she is with her own, she admits to seeing the breasts of many other women as somehow deficient. If our breasts are less than some hallowed ideal, we are not hearing about it from men, even if we're convinced it is what they're thinking. The outspoken critics here are ourselves, each other, and the in-our-face young vixens of Victoria's Secret.

The enemy is us.

If we took our cues from the entertainment and porn industries alone, we'd have to conclude that perfect boobs are big, firm, round as grapefruit halves, and attached to a slim, toned body. But with rare exceptions there is just one way to have huge firm breasts while otherwise wearing a size 2: implants.

Our fixation on such oxymoronic bodies was inaugurated by the nipple-less Barbie and endures as an ideal referred to by Kristen Harrison as "curvaceously thin." For Harrison, those words embody an irony akin to, say, "imposingly short" or "grossly petite." When it comes to prevailing notions of female body parts, the game is rigged: If we like our breasts, we surely must despise our asses. If, by some miracle of genetics and Pilates, our bellies are taut, we flaunt them at the expense of our R. Crumb thighs. A demurely tight tush is all too often juxtaposed with breasts no bigger than fried eggs.

We are blue-plate specials. You want the meatloaf; you're stuck with the succotash. But no matter how many times the waitress snarls, "No substitutes," we press on in our efforts to defy nature. I don't have the patience for the gym but I have plenty of friends who hire personal trainers and implore them to do what cardio, weight training, and breeding could not. "I don't like my ass." "Can you give me some definition in my waist?" Alas, there is no personal trainer, at any price, who can give you bigger boobs. If he or she succeeds in downsizing the rest of you, your boobs will retreat in tandem.

For my part, I have no clue how I ended up as an otherwise petite person with massive boobs. It just came on the plate, wedged between the hay fever, the eczema, and the world's slowest running time.

Though the phrase "Does size matter?" is so overused as to nauseate me, I was drawn nonetheless to the headline "Studies: Size Doesn't Matter," which, as evidenced by the smaller subtitle, managed not to be just about penises. In 2005 researchers addressing the American Psychological Society in Los Angeles shared the results of an MSNBC/*Elle* magazine online poll asking 50,000 women and heterosexual men how they felt about their own or their partners' breasts. While 70 percent of the women said they wanted fuller or rounder breasts, 56 percent of the men surveyed said they liked their partners' breasts just fine. There was more: women between eighteen and twenty-five years old were most likely to be content with their breasts (still just 33 percent), but 37 percent of them wanted bigger breasts. Of women in their twenties, 22 percent of the respondents were already concerned about "droopiness," and that number climbed steadily with age. Men, too, were on the alert for droopiness, and at least 20 percent (this number also increased with the subjects' age) said they found their partners' breasts "too droopy."

The interesting thing is that the study was reported as good news. This just in—men don't care about breast size! The story was picked up by news outlets around the world, the gist being that men aren't as shallow as we think. But why should this be so surprising? Why shouldn't the vast majority of men and women be satisfied with the breasts in their lives? Good news aside, there is the pesky matter of the 44 percent who would enhance their partners' breasts if they had a magic wand enabling them to do so. Ah, so these men will admit to an anonymous questionnaire what they wouldn't dare reveal to their partners. Speaking of wands, 85 percent of the women surveyed said they were happy with their partners' penis size. So, reading between the lines, I think it's safe to say that somewhere out there is a guy with a teensy penis who would prefer that his girlfriend had bigger tits.

That's just not fair.

One evening not long ago a group of women gathered in my home for a freewheeling discussion of breasts. They ranged in age from the early thirties to the late seventies. There were childless women, grandmothers, and mothers, one of them nursing her baby as we chatted. The women were straight and gay, with boobs of every size and heft. I billed the occasion as an "Our Boobs, Ourselves" party spiced by what I hoped would be lots of levity. To get everyone in the mood, I put a welcome sign on the door below a printout of Guinness World Record holder Maxi Mounds's Photo of the Week. Exploding from a bikini top apparently designed by Boeing, each of Maxi's boobs could have occupied its own kiddy pool.

The comedienne Kate Clinton once told me about a lesbian party game in which a bunch of women remove their tops and bras, form two lines, and face each other. Then they bend forward and jiggle their boobs while each takes a turn walking through. The game is called Car Wash. I love it: a group of women making gleeful fun of their own appendages. Men's fixations might spoil the fun, but when it's just us girls, boobs are hilarious, right?

Imagine my surprise, then, when the proceedings proved sober and serious. The guests told tales of frustration and weariness. Sally and Cate, the two oldest women, had bitter memories of having their breasts strapped tight to their chests by mothers intent on keeping them in check. At opposite ends of the scale, my fiftyish and stacked friend Susan recounted going "from nothing to everything" in what seemed like a week, while Madeline, now fifty-four, recalled waiting and waiting while what she believed were merely the preliminary contents of her first bra gave up the fight at an AA-cup. Cradling her baby girl, thirty-six-year-old KC said she didn't expect ever again to think of her boobs as anything but tired, sore milk dispensers.

At seventy-six, Sally was horrified that her breasts were actually getting bigger. "I have absolutely no use for these things," she said, cupping them disdainfully. "They serve no purpose whatsoever." I brought up the subject of finding a bra and the zaftig Susan started foaming at the mouth. She raged against

Warner's and Wacoal with the passion she once reserved for the military-industrial complex. "Why the hell should I pay seventy-five dollars for a minimizer? Where are the choices? It's a conspiracy!" Gorgeous Madeline has no boobs to speak of but her Kate Hepburn legs could break your heart. "I didn't care about that," she said. "All I wanted was big boobs."

"I come from a Greek family and we all have boobs," says large-breasted Cathy Halley, a thirty-eight-year-old editor of the website gURL.com. gURL has pages on, among other things, "being yourself," "beliefs," "sucky emotions," sports, dating, health, and sex. I tracked down Halley after reading gURL's "Boob Files," which include entry after telling entry from older women as well as the thirteen- to eighteen-year-olds the site targets. One, titled "Large," begins: "I have large breasts. They're not small, or medium. They're large. They're not on the small side of large or the large side of medium. They're just large. And they're not the kind that look large in a tight shirt or the kind that look large in a loose shirt. They're just large."

The writer, Naomi Odes, goes on to articulate how this state of affairs infects so many aspects of daily life. "Now, I've known this for a while, and yet people keep reminding me," she writes, "as if it's some sort of revelation. Boys in high school thought they were the first ones to discover it, so they had no problem screaming down the hallway, 'Hey you know something, you got big tits!' Thanks." Odes goes on to wax indignant over men who smile at her chest, bathing suit saleswomen, and bathing suit manufacturers. She concludes with the three words she must repeat like a mantra: "Leave me alone!"

Halley knows these feelings well. "I've thought about breast reduction, and people often suggest it. But I'm a purist: I don't dye my hair, I'm really ascetic in many ways. I don't even get expensive haircuts." But while Halley is just fine with herself, she admits to an adversarial relationship with the man on the street—make that, with the men on the street. "I'm trying to not lose my temper around men," she says. Once in San Francisco a man just reached over and cupped her breast. Halley lost it. "I was *so* angry, I started following him. I was screaming at him. He almost hit me, everybody in the street stopped, the buses stopped. I was just screaming." Halley has tried ignoring gawkers or spouting clever comebacks. She used to try to hide her boobs, but no more. As editor of gURL she hears from teenaged girls unused to the unwanted attention their breasts attract, who feel too conspicuous. The website responded by installing a Shockwave game in which players dodge or destroy catcallers. The game is called Street Hassle.

I spoke with David A. Frederick, who designed the MSNBC/*Elle* poll. Frederick is a graduate student in social psychology at the University of California–Los Angeles, arguably the body-dysmorphic-disorder capital of the world. "When we added the droopiness question, we were really surprised just how many women reported dissatisfaction," Frederick said. The corollary to this survey will be one in which women are asked whether their partners have ever suggested they get cosmetic surgery. What strikes Frederick is that so many women are getting implants that our perception of what is normal has shifted. All around us breasts are expanding, making our natural boobs appear smaller. At the same time, he'd like to learn to what extent fake boobs reflect negatively on a woman. What's the status of society's preoccupation with things that are "natural"? Is the earthy, "This is what forty looks like," unapologetically real woman defunct? In other words, has the curvaceously thin ideal overshadowed the trend toward women achieving a fit, healthy, proudly individual self?

When Dr. Harrison asked her students about their ideal body type they chose thinness over large breasts when the choice was presented in those terms. But Harrison knew the ideal body in today's mass media is not skinny and flat-chested; it's skinny and big-breasted. "So I created the body book," she said. With this flipbook of interchangeable body parts, Harrison encouraged young women to build their ideal body. And, to no one's surprise, most of the young women paired big boobs with slender frames. But Harrison, whose chief interest is how media influence and shape our desires, went on to correlate the results with the amount of television the women watched. And the correlation was clear: the more the women were exposed to television, the more they pined for the Barbie bod that rarely occurs in nature. "We're living in a media environment that defines the ideal body so narrowly, literally 36-24-36, and every girl is reminded of this hundreds of times a day," says Harrison. "She passes a billboard, reads a magazine—people are ambushed by this. It's the ubiquity of it; it's just endless and there's really no escape."

Sometimes I am in the mood to watch crappy television. On these occasions I will stray from the *Law & Order* franchise to partake of a cliché tale of spousal betrayal on Lifetime, or some offering of "action" or "suspense," these being commonly used terms for films that end with a fight to the death in an underground parking lot. So one Sunday I settled in to watch an installment of a miniseries titled *Category 7: The End of the World*.

Apparently the Apocalypse had gotten off to a running start in the premiere episode. Now all hell was about to break loose in Washington, D.C.—Chicago, New York, and Paris having already been obliterated—and only one woman could save the capital's terrified populace. This was a FEMA scientist played by Shannen Doherty. Watching her stomp around the Situation

Room with her perfectly highlighted hair whipping her face, I had two thoughts. First, this fictional Washington is in big trouble. Second, who knew FEMA stood for Federal Emergency Mammary Agency? Because the most notable feature of this woman—this supremely competent presidential appointee whose decisions bear directly on the survival of the planet—was, you guessed it, her breasts. They heaved upward and outward from the skimpy confines of a shirt I think I've seen in Victoria's Secret catalogs.

This is what Harrison means when she says the young consumers of such images are being ambushed.

I can see this needless torment in the eyes of my young friend Megan, who recently graduated from an all-women's college in Los Angeles. I've known Megan since she was a baby and have watched her evolve into a lovely young woman whose parents, by sending her to a women's college, hoped she would not be distracted or waylaid by the harsher dramas of coed living. But these women judged themselves so relentlessly that concern seems quaint. "We talked about boobs all the time," says Megan. A healthy, zaftig blonde of fierce intelligence, quick wit, and frank appetites, Megan describes her college as, for many of the women, a veritable temple of self-loathing. She says the plumbing was a mess as a result of epidemic bulimia. These are women who plan to become doctors, lawyers, policy makers, scholars, writers, and actors. Yet their academic dreams pale beside the desire to be beautiful and, most important, thin. Curvaceously thin, that is. Thin as rails, with boobs out to there. "My friend Esther always talks about getting implants, and she's got the best boobs," Megan tells me. "But she wants to get into Hollywood."

At the tender age of twenty-two, Megan avoids being on top during sex, or, if she is on top, she keeps her bra on. She cringes at the image of her 34D breasts, youthful and firm though they are, bouncing in full view of a man, even one she likes and trusts enough to have sex with. "My best friend's boobs are the same size as mine and she doesn't even need to wear a bra. Mine go all over the place and they have to be placed in a bra. We did topless line dancing at college, just the women, and I look at the pictures and I'm horrified," she says.

"I am one of the bigger-boob people among my friends," says Megan. "I can never wear tube tops and that's a pain. But they're not super big, so I can still hide them if I want. I do get mad if someone talks to them. I feel like I have to dress conservatively, wear a lot of button-down shirts. And there's at least one day a month when I can't leave my house simply because of my boobs."

Megan also admits to being confused about cleavage. "I've been watching a lot of *Sex and the City* reruns—I used to hate that show—and I realized something about boobs that drives me up the wall and makes me self-conscious about my size boobs," she says. "See, when the really skinny Hollywood women show cleavage, you get the impression it's tasteful and trendy. Even Julia Roberts didn't look that trashy in *Erin Brockovich*. But when someone with larger breasts who isn't skinny shows the same cleavage, it just signals to me that it's a trashy sort of look. So it's 'Smaller boob cleavage equals cute and classy. Large boob cleavage equals trailer-park trash.' And they are always wearing their bras when they have sex on top in *Sex and the City*. Maybe that's where I got it."

Of all the women I know, the one who is least self-effacing about her body is Alice, a riding instructor and horse trainer with size 38D breasts. Alice attributes her confidence to a decision she made when she was deep in debt with her horse barn. She became a stripper, working the lunch shift in an all-nude club in a South Shore suburb of Boston. Five feet, ten inches tall, with a bulky athletic frame, Alice was already thirty-five at the time. The job interview, such as it was, demanded nothing more than showing up.

"There was some art involved, but really, all you had to do was take your clothes off," Alice tells me. "Some girls could actually dance, but they were flat-chested. If you had anything in the way of boobs you could just fake it." Lap dances were particularly profitable, and the men were forbidden to lay a hand on her. Alice could up her tips by sticking her breasts in men's faces. Was she disgusted with herself? Did her self-esteem suffer?

Not one bit. "It was one of the most empowering, life-changing things I've ever done," says Alice, who gave herself the stage name Phoenixxx. "It was great for my ego. I felt sexy and guys everywhere totally picked up on it. You just radiate sex. And I gained the confidence I need to stand up in front of a class of students." Alice would strip naked in front of the lunch customers, but she soon learned that "all they care about is the boobs." As a horsewoman she's sometimes annoyed by her breasts, and it's been suggested that she should consider getting them reduced. "I couldn't do that," she says. "My boobs are a big part of my personality."

Of course Alice has a point (or two). Breasts don't make the woman—at least, I hope not. But she will be rewarded with a kind of peace and comfort if she befriends and embraces the breasts she's got. I can only wish for Megan that her confidence grows to rival Alice's, and sooner than later. As her mother's close friend, of course, I hope there are no lap dances involved.

The Riddle of the Rack

W HEN I WAS in third grade our class read Longfellow's epic poem *Evangeline,* of which I recall one detail. As the class read portions aloud by turns, it fell on disheveled, timid Stuie to read the stanza containing the word "bosom." As he stammered and hesitated, perhaps hoping against hope that Castro would bombard us with warheads before he had a chance to continue, the rest of the class lost it. BOSOM!!! Ha ha ha ha ha! What the hell did we know? It was as if we were being asked to calmly recite a paean to doody.

In our prepubescent hysterics not one of us girls gave a thought to the fact that someday we, too, would possess this universally embarrassing item. Any mention of "tits" or "boobies" could turn my complexion instantly purple. But secretly I had good and wholesome feelings about the word "bosom." I found it old-fashioned and comforting; it was a word I'd heard my grandmother and my great-aunts say, as in "Honey, that dress accentuates your lovely bosom." A bosom was what mothers and grandmothers possessed. A bosom, the fuller the better, was a hallmark of nurturing. Well into my teen years,

I would burrow into my mother's bosom when we made up after a fight. When we're relaxing in front of the television, my eight-year-old stepgranddaughter absentmindedly places her head on my bosom and takes refuge there.

It has occurred to me that in the course of human evolution, what was once a bosom, nonsexual and compelling only to the nursing and very young, somehow became an anatomical feature prized by men, and an erogenous zone for women. Somewhere along the line, the bosom became the rack; the teat became the tit: "nice tits." At some point women came to prize their breasts as a means of giving and receiving sexual pleasure as well as of offering maternal sustenance. No one knows for certain how this came to pass, or why.

A breast is simply a cluster of glands encased in fat. With the progesterone production that comes at puberty, the breasts awaken from their childhood slumber and begin to grow. They may keep developing for as long as four years. No matter how petite, a breast consists of fifteen to twenty lobes of glandular tissue. The lobes themselves encase thousands of tiny glands called alveoli. Like grapes, these are joined by a series of ducts that produce milk during lactation. Each lobe feeds into a single conduit to the nipple, behind which the ducts expand to form small reservoirs called lactiferous sinuses, each less than a tenth of an inch wide. The glandular tissue is cushioned by fat and connective tissue encased in skin, with the whole business connected to the chest wall by ligaments. These are the infamous Cooper's ligaments, which, as they grow weary with age, bring us the dreaded "Cooper's droop."

And this is the sum total of the geography of the breast: an arguably inelegant sack of fat wrapped around some milk ducts, milk glands, and blood vessels, wrapped in skin and crowned with a nipple. This is what all the fuss, the longing, the envy and heartache are all about. An A-cup breast weighs about a quarter of a pound, a B-cup half a pound. A D-cup weighs a pound or more. Our nipples can point up or down, left or right. Nearly all women's breasts are asymmetrical. And no matter how much we lift weights or flap our arms like a bird, the shape of our breasts is dictated by our genes and body fat. A woman's membership in the Itty Bitty Titty Committee is a done deal before she is born.

Eventually all breasts will undergo ptosis—sagging, to you. As we age, our breasts lose the firming protein known as collagen. Our milk glands, now having little more than sentimental value, shrink and retreat. And where they retreat, fat, which abhors a vacuum, moves in. Though there are few caricatures more infuriating than the cartoon granny with her tits around her knees, our skin is fated to lose its elasticity with age; as the breast envelope weakens, our boobs grow tired and yield to gravity.

Subject to the vagaries of hormones that surge and retreat monthly and as we age, the cells that constitute breasts big and small are one of the body's prime sites for mutations that lead to cancer. Breast cancer is still poorly understood; the specter of it has us submitting to routine mammograms in constant dread of being the one out of eight women who, if we live long enough, will eventually get the disease. I recently remarked to my mild-mannered gynecologist, "You know, women my age only come to you every year to find out if we have cancer or not." "Oh," he replied, "why that's just . . . My God! You're right!"

Among our earliest ancestors, did breasts do double time as tits? Did men hold forth with prelinguistic grunts at the sight of a really nice set of, oh, boulders? We're the only primates whose breasts don't go flaccid and recede when we're not pregnant or lactating. But our breast tissue is mostly fat, not milk glands. What selective advantage nudged evolution in this direction?

Did a pair of engorged breasts, preoccupied though they were with nursing a child, nonetheless ignite a spate of caveman erections? For what purpose did breasts evolve into another of the body's fat repositories? Do bodily proportions affect primal longings so much that bigger boobs afford women a reproductive edge? And if so, what are we to make of my flat-chested friends Sara, Madeline, and Vivian, not to mention the female population of Japan? If "ideal" bust-to-waist-to-hip ratio means a better shot at reproductive success and survival, how come there continues to be such a surfeit of really funny-shaped people? To what should we attribute the hardy survival of people with no asses, or women like a certain aunt of mine, whose shape makes her look as if she's standing in a barrel?

Though evolutionary theorists have well-reasoned explanations for all kinds of things, the matter of breasts, and men's attraction to them, nags at them still. They are nearly as baffled as I am. Of course, any feature in adult animals that distinguishes one sex from the other is felt to be sexually attractive, says the anthropologist Elaine Morgan, the author of *The Descent of Woman*. "Sometimes, as in the peacock's tail, they become exaggerated by what Darwin called sexual selection. Such exaggeration is more common in males than females, though. Female birds and mammals are usually drabber, in the interests of safety, to blend into the background and not attract the attention of predators while sitting on the nest."

If breasts evolved as the human female's plumage, going against type, they must have triggered many a misunderstanding among prehistoric singles. As one researcher noted, shouldn't pendulous breasts have been sexually repulsive, at least initially? They signal that a woman has no current reproductive potential—in today's parlance, she's unavailable. So wouldn't larger-than-normal breasts signal to prehistoric

Don Juans to back off please, this girl has already got her hands full?

Perhaps the plump-breasted woman was a turnoff only to dominant males. Some biologists have argued that it was in early woman's survival interest to avoid being just another babe in a dominant's male's harem. Noticeably bigger breasts might have been helpful in this regard, if the dominant males concluded that their possessor was sexually unavailable. The amply endowed female could then team up with and enjoy the more focused attentions of a nondominant male. What confounds biologists is how the male of the species evolved to assess what scientists call a woman's "mate value." I'm not talking about her worth in cows, diamonds, or spa visits, but her fitness for breeding. In natural selection that is the whole point, and the only point: to propagate the species. But the traits that make women good breeders—their fertility, their resistance to disease, even their age—can elude males looking for a suitable mate. The reproductive value of men was evident through their status in the clan, while a woman's reproductive value is, for the most part, concealed. So biologists assume that, in a time in the almost inconceivable past, a time before foundation, antiwrinkle potions, hair dye, and Botox, men grew attuned to the attributes we now call attractive. Plump breasts, a narrow waist, and broad hips were the best available indicators of a woman's good health and mate value.

When it comes to evolution-based theories of mate selection, the notion of good looks is not frivolous. For evolutionary scientists "attractiveness" is not a slippery, eye-of-the-beholder term. And contemporary studies have consistently shown that breast size and waist-to-hip ratio—otherwise known as a girl's "measurements"—reveal, on a primal level, what mate-seeking males need to know. This is true across cultures and in spite of prevailing fashions. It's true in cultures that like their women slender and in far-flung locales such as Mali and Niger, where many young brides are still force-fed to the point of obesity.

But this still doesn't explain why big breasts evolved, or why men remain fixated on them. And if plump breasts are a banner of reproductive fitness in mate selection, why are men more attracted to women who are otherwise slender? Stick-thin marathoners and anorexics often stop menstruating altogether, while plump women have estrogen to spare. And the rail-thin, huge-busted woman is an artifact of the implant age, which dawned just fifty years ago. This woman may thrive in the Victoria's Secret catalog, but she does not exist in nature.

In 1995, members of the Human Evolution and Behavior Society convened at Binghamton University, of which I happen to be an alumna. Professor Edward Miller presented a paper entitled "Breasts: Their Evolutionary Origins as a Deceptive Signal of Need for Provisioning and Temporary Infertility." Miller, whose field is economics, poses the question, Why are men attracted to breasts? If men couldn't distinguish breasts that were big with fatty tissue from breasts plump with glandular tissue, the evolutionary theorists have to come up with a selective advantage other than that of a woman's increased capacity to nurse and nurture her young. When Miller writes that flat-chested women were "unable to attract as much male investment, and thus their genes died out," I suppose he's talking about females whose breasts were nearly identical to those of males.

It's even been suggested that male attraction to big breasts is the genetically programmed result of the disappearance of a gene for male repulsion from big breasts. A gene for male repulsion from big breasts? Those were the days. Miller's theory may be confusing, but his basic premise makes sense to me. He believes that lactating females with swollen breasts required more "provisioning," which is academy-talk meaning that they had to eat more. In a nutshell, Miller concludes that breasts originated as a "deceptive signal" of the need for a hearty meal. The males who offered up the meat were rewarded, like bonobos, with copulation. And the females were more likely to stick with the guy bringing home the bacon, or the mastodon, than with one who was turned off by big breasts and bolted into the bush. And this big boob–big provider pair, bonded by a woman's hunger for food and a man's hunger for sex, would have more, and healthier babies. And these would be babies of the big-boob mother, with the resulting girls more likely to be large-breasted themselves.

Says Miller: "The mechanism is simple. Extra provisioning is in the female's reproductive interests at all times, not merely when she is lactating. A female with breast fat deposits appears attractive to men and receives extra provisioning." And a better-fed female produces more live offspring. Evolutionary biologists also believe the shift of fat to the breasts imposed "no major costs." Easy for them to say. Or perhaps it was true before the beneficiaries of this fat migration were forced to pay $100 or more for a bra that actually fits.

My flattest friends notwithstanding, I like Miller's theory, not just because I can wrap my brain around it, but because it illuminates the intuitive notion that our ancestors were most likely to lust after women with some meat on their bones.

Meanwhile, apart from their appearance, how did breasts evolve to deliver so much erotic pleasure to women themselves? Talk to some ardent feminists and activists for going topless, and they will say the matter is not up for debate: breasts are not sexual organs. Though some men appear confused about this concept, we know the breasts are not literally sex organs, essential to natural reproduction. There are just two of those, one for each sex, and even people who can't name them can

point to them. But what about the breast as a sexual feature of
the anatomy? Whether the deed was done as a result of men's
connivance or nature's wisdom, how can anyone deny that
breasts are sexual?

Desmond Morris had it all figured out, as he explained in his
longtime bestseller *The Naked Ape*. In that book and ensuing
ones Morris puts forward an evolutionary theory that seems to
take breasts' sexual nature into account. He wrote that the
breasts most likely developed to mimic the buttocks. It's generally believed that humans advanced—or regressed, depending
on one's tastes—from doggie-style copulation to full frontal in-
tercourse. He reasons that, as the buttocks became less of a
come-hither sexual signal, males favored females whose boobs
looked as inviting as a nice plump behind. Simultaneously, it's
easy to imagine that the increasing erotic sensitivity of breasts
would encourage women's interest in full frontal sex, too. So
big boobs evolved to make sex sexier, and in the natural selection business, sexier sex is forever in the credits column.

This theory infuriates many. In her touché tract *The Descent
of Woman*, Morgan has this to say about Desmond Morris's
fleshy hemispheres: "Good stuff, but hard to take seriously.
Wolf packs manage to cooperate without all this exotic para-
phernalia. Our near relatives the gibbons remain faithful for life
without personalized frontal sex, without elaborate erogenous
zones. . . . Why couldn't we?" Morgan doesn't buy Morris's
circular argument, "I find this attribute sexy: therefore it must
have evolved in order that I might find it sexy." That, she points
out, is "like saying that a woman walks with a wiggle because
this is attractive to a male. In fact, she only walks with a wiggle
because her children are intelligent. The necessity of passing a
large-skulled infant's head through her pelvic ring has prevented
her skeleton from adapting to bipedalism quite as gracefully as

that of her brothers; and males only find this defect attractive because they associate it with femininity." So there.

In her repudiation of Morris—silly, *silly* man—Morgan reminds us that when it comes to breasts, "it would be reasonable to think about the primary beneficiary of the process—namely, the baby—rather than trying to relate it to the child's father's occupation." In order to nurse her babies, the evolving, now hairless human female needed "a lump of something less bony, something pliant and of a convenient size for small hands to grab hold of while you, the baby, lie on her lap and guide your lips to the right place. . . . And since you are what evolution is all about, what you need you ultimately get. You get two lovely pendulous dollopy breasts, as easy to hold on to as a bottle." Fatty breasts have other advantages, too. According to the late anthropologist Lila Leibowitz, the fat may have evolved to cushion the breast's more fragile underlying tissue and help keep the mother's milk warm. Elaine Morgan believes that today's breasts—my DDDs, for example—might owe their shape to more recent developments, like an increase in dietary protein and improved physical fitness regimens, and they are maintained by better supporting and well-fitting brassieres.

But the answer is, really, No one knows.

Nineteenth-century practitioners of anthropometry, the pseudoscientific study of human body proportions, exalted the breast, above all else, as the essence of womanhood. In 1858 Jules Michelet wrote in his treatise *L'Amour* that a woman's breathing produced the unique feminine undulation of the bosom, which "expresses all her sentiments in a mute eloquence." As Stephen Kern writes in *Anatomy and Destiny,* the German critic Leo Berg speculated in an 1891 treatise that the breast alone determined a woman's entire personality. "A woman's breast is the organ with which she is able to express herself most intelligently.

It is her language and poetry, her history and her music, her purity and her desire . . ." Gevalt!

A tit man if there ever was one, Berg declared that "the bosom is the central organ of all female ideas, wishes and moods." And one of Berg's contemporaries, a physician, gushed that the "Caucasian female bust" is "the crowning act, the most elaborate and most perfect form and model of beauty, human eyes have yet beheld." (A woman might not choose this particular doctor for her annual breast exam.) Both men's statements reflect an obsession with breasts that continues to mystify those who study the subject with more rigor and less lust.

"I think breast obsession is partly cultural," Elaine Morgan told me. "It varies between different cultures and it varies over time. In some Oriental peoples, breasts seem to be smaller than they currently appear in the West, and as long as they were isolated from Western influences [breasts] didn't seem to be given the same priority as sexual signals. Other things, like bound feet, were felt to be more sexually exciting. In the heyday of the bustle, it was the curve of the buttocks that was being exaggerated."

One would assume that in cultures where woman habitually go bare-breasted, everyday exposure to breasts would make them less sexualized. But even in these cultures, beautiful breasts are objects of admiration and envy, if not unbridled lust. Nancy Etcoff writes in *Survival of the Prettiest* that, bare-breasted or not, cultures around the world distinguish three categories of breasts. These can be mimed by putting one's palms flat against one's chest, pointing the hands straight out from the chest, or angling one's hands downward from the chest. The first sketches an infertile young girl, the second a nubile young woman. The third conveys a woman who has given birth and nursed a child, or an older woman whether she has nursed or not.

I've been corresponding with Devendra Singh, a psychologist at the University of Texas in Austin. Dr. Singh has done numerous studies of what attracts men to women, studies I love because they offer stark confirmation of what a 32DDD already knows. For example, in one study the male subjects, presented with a series of pictures, rated younger women more attractive than older ones. But when the older women's pictures were altered to include big breasts, they instantly became a whole lot more attractive, even more than young, lovely women with flat chests.

Singh is best known for his cross-cultural studies. From India's Rubenesque Brahmin matriarchs to the slender herdswomen of the Masai, the waist-to-hip ratio of females whom males consider most attractive stays surprisingly consistent. In studies of men from the Azores, Guinea-Bissau, Indonesia, and the United States the hourglass figure prevailed. And here's the thing—if the few studies on the subject are to be taken seriously, there appear to be fewer and fewer places on the planet where big boobs aren't a turn-on. Yes, Chinese men have a traditional fixation on tiny feet, while in African and Caribbean cultures women are admired for plump buttocks. And some men like their women wide and some narrow. But the global infiltration of Western media has Asian men worked up over women with serious jugs, and sales of breast-enhancement products that promise to indulge them are booming. In some cultures and subcultures, this truth runs counter to intuition, of course. I'll never forget one morning in the lingerie department of Macy's in Manhattan, where I happened upon a gaggle of Chasidic men, replete with payess and tefillin, purchasing lacy push-up bras. As the Fugs put it so memorably, everybody likes boobs-a-lot.

Singh concludes, "Female figures with slender bodies, low waist-to-hip ratios, and large breasts were rated as most attractive, feminine looking, healthy and desirable for both casual and long-term relationships. It seems that larger body size, a high waist-to-hip ratio, and larger hips made the female figures appear older, unattractive and less desirable for engaging in romantic relationships." My own, blatantly unscientific polling bears this out. I have been groped, grabbed, tweaked, and hooted at in locales as culturally diverse as North Africa, the Middle East, India, Spain, Greece, the British Isles, the Czech Republic, Central America, and Newfoundland. (If my findings are accurate, the planet's ground zero of breast lust is a certain café in the port of Brindisi, Italy.) A British study of men in the UK and Kenya yielded similar results. The British preferred their women slighter, which at least for me invites the question: What's with the bacon crispies and mayonnaise piled on chips, and with the compulsion to drown layer cake in heavy cream?

Recently a wizened man in his nineties came on to me. He asked my name and inquired whether I had a husband. And I'm certain that, while he inched along at a snail's pace and had trouble recalling where he'd put the glasses that jutted from his shirt pocket, he knew exactly what he was doing when he managed to brush against my breasts. And why not? As a male friend of mine is fond of saying, where there's life there's hope. On the other hand, you can bet that a man hurtling toward the century mark has lost interest in many, maybe most, of the things that captivated him in his youth. And yet, here were my boobs, thrusting forth into his visual field, ever shrinking as it succumbed to macular degeneration.

And what does such a man do with these boobs? He desires them. If he can get away with it, he cops a feel. We may never grasp exactly why, but it has to be in his genes. And, of course, in ours.

The Perfect Bra

THE SEARCH FOR the perfect bra is in many ways akin to the quest for enlightenment. You may come close, but odds are you will never quite get there. On your journey, you will encounter many wise people, and you will learn from them. Others may lead you astray with hollow, ultimately cruel promises, such as "One size fits all." As you make your ascent, you will hand over your Visa card for increasingly pricey incarnations of what you once, in your youthful ignorance, assumed to be a simple undergarment.

When Dorothy Parker remarked that "brevity is the soul of lingerie," she was obviously unfamiliar with the prevailing selection of bras for women burdened with DDD boobs. Bras in my size are often hideous and rarely cheap. An exception to the latter rule is the underwire 32DDD I picked up at the Sample Road flea market, my favorite stop when I visit my parents in south Florida. I didn't try the bra on, but it was actually my size, or so the tag said. Everything seemed in order: it had two cups and hooked in the back; it cost five dollars. I figured how could I go wrong. Let us count the ways. The cups were too close together, creating the boob equivalent of crossed eyes. Each cup came to a scary point. The ersatz spandex sliced into my armpits. This was a hair shirt masquerading as a bra.

Another memorable bra was a minimizer I picked up at Filene's. A minimizer is, of course, a bra that minimizes, as opposed to a bra that is too tight. Fine line there; would anyone, I wonder, be seduced into buying "minimizer" shoes? Since it was so hard to find bras in my size, I wore them to death. This one announced its demise by extruding its underwire into my soft flesh, leaving a set of neat wounds like misplaced stigmata. Bras have exploded off me for no reason. A saleswoman at an old-fashioned ladies' apparel shop in Orleans, Massachusetts, convinced me I required something called a baseball bra, a sports bra with baseball-style stitching that promised to minimize to such an extent I should've been suspicious right off the bat, so to speak. I have taken enough physics to know that matter can be neither created nor destroyed. I bought the bra, of course. The first and only day I wore it, the circulation in my chest was so fiercely curtailed that my ribs ached and my breasts went completely numb. The effect lasted a while. I could've had my nipples pierced without flinching.

Show me a bra that's comfortable and really truly fits, and I'll pay . . . hmmm. Well, apparently, I'll pay $150 to $200. I acquired my first really expensive bra at La Petite Coquette on University Place in downtown Manhattan. I had so much fun in there, trying on bras in a lush, pillowy harem room and girl-bonding with the saleswomen. They made me feel like I deserved nothing less than the best: my 32DDDs were, of course, high maintenance and must be coddled like a childhood infirmity. Would I scrimp on a mattress after back surgery? Well, this was the same thing, and could I also have something sexy as hell, if possible? I strode out of that store feeling like one hot tamale. With a satisfied spring in my step, I advanced toward Fifth Avenue flashing my illicit-looking La Petite Coquette bag and thinking, Oh, aren't you all dying to know what's nestled in that red tissue paper. But after about ten blocks the euphoria wore off, replaced by something like a bludgeon to the forehead: "You just forked over a hundred fifty dollars . . . for a *bra*!"

But what a bra. I flashed it to my friend Barbara at dinner that evening, and offered viewings after that to a succession of friends, a few of them male. Without exception each exclaimed: "Oh, my God!" Said bra is a confection of crimson and black lace, which curls its way up the straps to conceal how clinically wide they are. Nestled in this Ferrari of undergarments, my breasts are enviably sumptuous. They thrust upward and outward so deliciously I myself am enthralled at my own reflection. I want to wear this bra over my clothing, not under it. And my friends didn't bat an eyelash when I revealed the price. Well, that's what a decent bra costs, they said. Huh? How come nobody told *me*? Since it wasn't until middle age that I began seeing my breasts as assets rather than liabilities, I didn't lavish on them the money or attention I spent on, for example, my feet; in fact, I often settled for whatever I could unearth in the bargain bin. These bras didn't fit; they were uncomfortable and either smashed my breasts to mesas or left them flapping in the breeze. As I reinvented myself as a Gypsy, a wilderness babe, an understated collegian, it never occurred to me that a decent bra would enhance my appearance.

I remember my first bra. The memory is a painful one because the bra was a castoff, once white but turned gray from too many washings, and it would've been none too attractive in any color. It was what they called a training bra, which the boys joked was a normal bra with two wheels attached to it.

I fished the bra out of a bag of clothing consigned to the attic by my sister, who is five years older than I. The bra was my secret. I'd model it for myself in front of the mirror and fantasize that I actually had something, however infinitesimal, to add a bulge to its cathedral-window-shaped panels. I was in the seventh grade. The problem was, I was ten. I needed a bra as much as a boy needs Tampax.

There were a few other girls, also ahead of themselves in school, who still wore undershirts. But their numbers were dwindling fast. In the ravages of puberty, the gangly, acne-pocked boys in our class took notice. "Are you a turtle?" the boys would ask. Then they'd tug once on your bra strap. "Then how come you snap?"

One morning I went to school to discover that the clique of last holdouts had crossed over in unison. They all wore white blouses, through each of which I could clearly see a bra's unmistakable contours. I immediately felt like vomiting, which was my reaction to stress in those days. How could this have happened? I would be the very last girl at Woodland Junior High School to don a bra, which I resolved to do the very next day.

I'm sure now that I was underestimating her, but at the time I assumed if I told my mother she'd moan, "Oh please. You? A bra?" So I wore the battered hand-me-down, day after day, slipping it off as soon as I got home, until my mother finally intercepted me. Like the prepubescent I was, I wept, I gurgled, my nose ran. And then we went bra shopping. It's one of my most powerful memories: marching up to the training-bra section of Macy's and choosing from among the boxes a white-as-snow bra with lacy stretch cups and a pink bow at the spot that would, someday, mark my cleavage. Never mind that I kicked the other kids' asses in algebra and French. Fastened absurdly around my chest, which was still flat as a sheet of oak tag, that bra was a badge of belonging and girlhood like nothing pre-ceding it.

Little did I know, or care to consider at the time when I ached with envy at the other girls' tiny twin bumps, that some-day I'd leave them all in the dust.

And that is my last clear bra memory of my youth. How did I manage in the ensuing years? I faintly recall a padded Cross Your Heart model in an A-cup, but that couldn't have lasted long. I remember shopping expeditions to Orbach's and Gim-bels for bathing suits, school dresses, and winter coats. I have memories of choosing among styles of underpants. But my pro-curement of bras in increasingly bigger sizes is one big blank.

My actual adult bra size was revealed to me as I prepared for my first wedding. I was twenty-eight and did not take well to the fuss surrounding the event and me. My mother made an ap-pointment for us at Laura Ashley, which stunned me because, for one thing, I was having a small backyard ceremony and I expected to wear something simple and comfortable; for an-other, I wasn't aware that short Jewish girls were *allowed* to shop at Laura Ashley. After jamming myself into several itchy, poofy dresses that made me feel like a cross between the good witch Glinda and a drag queen, I declared, Enough. While my mother sat in the idling car, I ran into Bloomingdale's and bought an ivory lace shift with a satin slip.

I was pretty damned proud of myself until I realized the slip had spaghetti straps and my bra straps would show. For those of you born decades later, I should explain that there was a time when it was widely considered unacceptable to walk around with half your bra showing. In olden times, an exposed bra strap was akin to gunk on one's teeth or toilet paper trailing from one's shoe. A kindly female stranger would tap you on the shoulder and say, "Your *strap* is showing," and you'd duck into the nearest ladies' room (that's what they were called in the Eisenhower years) and pull yourself together. And in these pre-goth, pre-Madonna days you didn't venture out in public wearing a black bra with a see-through white top unless you were insane.

The wedding dress required a strapless bra. I'm still unclear on this concept. And I was even more baffled to learn from the mother hen at the corset shop that my bra size was 32DDD, and that indeed she could provide a strapless bra in that size. I had studied science in college. Force equals mass times gravity, all that stuff. Wasn't a size 32DDD strapless bra as flawed as a suspension bridge with no suspension? My breasts must have weighed several pounds each. How tight would this bra have to be to create a sturdy shelf for them?

My mother bought me the bra, until then the most expensive I'd ever owned. I wore it precisely once, at the wedding. It hovered in place as we exchanged vows, and started inching south shortly after. During the first hora it landed around my ankles. At the same time my dyed-to-match heels collapsed and, after I removed those, my $30 pantyhose were ripped to shreds. By the time we cut the cake, the outfit was kaput. The marriage lasted just slightly longer.

I have a drawer so overstuffed with bras I occasionally lose one or two to the jaws of my dresser's dark netherworld. It is difficult to dispose of a garment that is lovely, sexy even when unoccupied, and set you back at least $50. It is hard to admit that once again you knowingly shelled out good money for a bra you didn't bother trying on. Or worse, you tried it on and wanted it so badly you chose to ignore the way it made you spring a set of auxiliary boobs, hovering in front of each armpit. So badly did you want that sex kitten effect only achievable in matching bra and panties that, assuming your least chubby pose in the dressing room mirror, you convinced yourself it was the erotic appeal of this ensemble, and not the unsuitable dimensions of the bra itself, that took your breath away.

In my personal hall of shame, bra mistakes are second only to shoe mistakes. But shoes I can pass along to my friends or virtuously deposit at the swap shop. A bum bra is a more private blunder. Why do I save them? Under what circumstances might my boobs shrink an entire cup size to fit that scallop-edged violet push-up bra? I don't linger over that drawer because it makes me feel too guilty.

I wish I'd known about the Bra Ball while it was in progress. Emily Duffy, a San Francisco artist internationally known for her art cars, began accepting bra donations in 1993. Over the next decade she hooked the bras together to form a ball similar to the kind children make from rubber bands. Containing 18,085 bras, the finished Bra Ball measures five feet in diameter and weighs over 1,800 pounds.

As word of the Bra Ball spread, thanks to the Internet and radio and television coverage, bras flooded in from everywhere. Duffy found herself inundated with lacy or prim castoffs from women in Canada, France, Germany, Brazil, Japan, India, and Serbia. The letters accompanying the mostly brand-new bras told tale after tale of physical discomfort and money ill spent. Duffy shared some of the letters with me. My favorite is from a woman in Yokohama, Japan: "I think bra is necessary and very precious for female but I have become no wear bra recently at home. Because of comfortable."

In the lexicon of the lingerie trade I am a "full-figured woman." Never mind that where I'm narrow I'm as narrow as an arrow; what matters is that I'm more than broad where a broad should be broad. I have been blessed, or cursed, with both a rare blood type and a rare bra size. To accommodate a

32DDD, or a European 32E, is feasible but requires more effort than the usual dash into Macy's. I resent this. I resent it not only because my bra size confounds salesclerks in even the best-stocked foundations departments, but because bras my size, when I locate them, cost at least twice as much as bras for normal women. Never mind that spending $100 on a bra that actually fits is ultimately more economical than buying three bras that don't at $45 a pop. It's the concept that unnerves me. Put simply, if I spend $100 on something I would like that something to be earrings.

An anonymous and equally endowed sister who contributes to a blog titled everything2.com echoes my outrage: "It's virtually impossible for me to go to a store and buy a bra that fits me. I remember walking into Victoria's Secret a few months ago for the first time to buy myself some nice bras, and leaving ten minutes later in tears. What happened was:

Me: Can you show me where you keep the larger sizes?

Clerk: What size are you looking for?

Me: (blushing, in a very tiny voice) Size . . . 34 . . . E?

Clerk (blinks and stares at me . . . then bursts into uncontrollable laughter.)

Me (turns and walks back out, crying)."

A bra is a complex artifact. If you doubt this, have a look at the diagrams accompanying brassiere patent applications in the century and a half since the bra declared its independence from the corset. You'd conclude that these gizmos were designed by Lockheed engineers in their spare time, and you would not be far off. The bra poses engineering challenges unrivaled by another other garment. Consider this: A workable bra must battle gravity on two fronts while being as inconspicuous as possible. It must separate as well as lift without constricting movement about the shoulders and armpits. It must stretch as well as retract; it must be forgiving and adjustable; it must not stifle the circulation, leave bruises, or cause lacerations after long hours of wear. A woman has every right to expect to dance, skip, stretch, and bend without her bra straps defecting to her upper arms, or one or both of her boobs breaking free. The bra must meet all these requirements while somehow managing to be attractive, if not downright sexy.

Though you can read entertaining accounts of his purported accomplishments, sadly, the great Otto Titzling is fictional. There was no eureka moment. The structure of the bra as we know it did not come to its inventor in an opium dream. With respect to breast support, history advanced two steps forward, one step back over the centuries. Just when it seemed that boobs would be allowed to breathe, they endured yet another suffocating backlash in the name of changing fashions and morals.

"The bra is a keener pleasure for being optional," observed the fashion historian Anne Hollander, a petite, lovely, and infinitely classy woman who joined me for afternoon tea in her Washington Square neighborhood. "Thirty years ago, many items once necessary to female life," such as corsets and girdles, were "banished to the torture chamber of the patriarchy. One by one, they have all come back, licensed frivolities rather than slavish concessions to the male beholder." In fact, since the latter years of the twentieth century, bras have been designed more and more to enhance women's freedom rather than stifle it. Witness the sports bra, and all the bras with, as Hollander put it, "no function but to delight," with both wearer and remover complicit in the bra's true purpose.

Coming of age in the late sixties, I was witness to the frenzy to shed bras altogether. But I never joined in that chorus. I've almost never gone braless. When you've got boobs as big as mine, not wearing a bra is as liberating as walking barefoot on gravel. I like bras and owe my daily comfort and postoperative spinal health to them. And I prefer looking all put-together. Working or lounging at home, I select from a wardrobe of soft lint-colored leggings and oversized tees all washed to near translucency. But when I step out, even if it's to run to the general store, I get "dressed," meaning I put on jeans and a shirt my size. Though I'll never approach her Old World style and elegance, I agree with Hollander, who always wears heels, that when it comes to being out and about in the world, too much comfort makes us look like infants. When it comes to style, "comfort is of no interest and never has been," sniffed Hollander, my one meeting with whom left me feeling that I must urgently drop fifty pounds and shun all synthetic knits. But in the bra department I want both things: I want to look smart and I want to be spared the feeling that someone is continually pouring acid on my shoulders. Is this possible, at any cost? If only I could find it, the perfect bra. But first, some history.

As early as 2000 B.C., the women of Crete wore a corset that supported their breasts at the base and thrust them upward and out. About a thousand years later, that corset had morphed into a strip of cloth rolled below the breasts. Over time, the cloth strip grew wider and was wrapped not just below the breasts, but also over them. Each subtle innovation had a new and unappealing name: the *anamaskhaliter,* the *mastodeton.* The early Romans cinched their breasts with bandages called *fascia.* Fuller-breasted women had an alternative in the boob-squishing *mamillare,* a soft leather bra, and others wore the *strophium,* a scarf that gently enfolded the breasts rather than smashing them into submission. In the Roman Empire women with soft pendulous breasts were considered barbaric, and various thinkers of the day—thinkers of the male variety, that is—were on record with concoctions to keep the breasts small. Dioscorides, a physician and botanist, advised women to dredge their *fascia* in the powdered stone of Naxos. Pliny prescribed grinder's mud. Ovid promoted the use of breadcrumbs dipped in milk.

According to Beatrice Fontanel's *Support and Seduction: A History of Corsets and Bras,* when the Roman Empire fell a large proportion of boobs did, too. Women of the conquering Celts and Germans let their breasts submit to gravity under loose tunics. Breast binding returned in the Gothic period, and from the fourteenth century on breasts have been bound, bandaged, corseted, and otherwise imprisoned. From the Middle Ages into the early Renaissance, breasts were tamed with laced corsets and bodices. While the Church was scornful of the slightest flash of ankle, necklines plunged, décolletage heaved shamelessly. Fontanel quotes a Medieval romance: "And if her paps be too heavy, let her bind her breast with cloth."

The Renaissance was a celebration of the feminine form, if not women's rights. Creamy pert breasts, usually no bigger than the requisite handful, appear in painting after painting. Portraits of women depict them posed demurely at their dressing tables, breasts peeking through transparent wraps, or lounging with one breast uncovered. With upswept hair, women shared their loveliest assets—the ripe cleavage, the exposed collarbone, the nape of the neck. But as the Renaissance receded, women's costumes expanded, stiffened, and clamped down in unfortunate ways. Once again, boobs were sentenced to indefinite confinement in bodices with busks crafted of such cuddly materials as boxwood, ivory, silver, and for those on a budget, turkey cartilage. Witness those seventeenth-century portraits of women with no discernible bosoms, their necks lost inside ruffs so wide the effect is as if the women's heads are being served on a platter.

For years, physicians spoke out against the corset, the physical cruelty of which sometimes surfaced in their practices when female patients suffered serious injuries to the internal organs. Fontanel writes that the corset put too much pressure against the stomach and compressed the solar plexus "to the point where women fainted at the drop of a hat." For women of those times, the opportunity to loosen one's corset straps was as delicious as, for women of my mother's generation, the moment of peeling off the long-line girdle in exchange for a muumuu. Fontanel quotes a sign in the window of a corsetmaker's shop promising a product that "contains the strong, sustains the weak, and brings back those who have strayed." One might use these precise words to sell muzzles for dogs.

In his "cultural history of the human body," *Anatomy and Destiny,* Stephen Kern writes that during the late nineteenth century the call for women's clothing reform amplified as doctors and physical culture advocates studied the damage done by tightly laced corsets. In 1856 the Englishwoman Roxey Caplan urged that the corset be redesigned with physiology in mind. As Kern writes, "She then listed twenty-three different kinds of corsets suited to different needs: for infants and young girls, for the corpulent, for girls who grow too rapidly, for pregnancy, even to prevent children from standing on one leg." Caplan also struck fear in the hearts of pale provincial European women by reminding them that shedding their corsets altogether would lead to the sagging common among African tribal women whose breasts, she warned, "hung so low that they could nurse infants by flinging their breasts over their shoulders or under their arms."

But not all those designing breast accoutrements in the late

1890s were weighing the clinical merits of corsets loose or tight. Around this time, indulging a fleeting fashion statement, expensive Parisian jewelry shops were offering something called *anneaux de sein,* or bosom rings. A ring was inserted through each nipple, and in some daring women a delicate chain connected the two. The effect, which foretold today's parade of the pierced and tattooed, enlarged the breasts slightly and, as Kern notes, "kept them in a state of constant excitation."

Thanks to Madonna and the folks at Frederick's, corsets and bustiers are still widely available. But in glorious contrast to their original purpose, they are now worn mainly for the purpose of being removed, preferably with the help of a willing accomplice, and as soon as possible. You don't see too many long-line bras around these days. My mother had a collection of these, which she wore along with a panty girdle that, to my touch, seemed to be steel-reinforced. When I was little I'd watch her grimace as she slipped her dress over this cruel ensemble. "So Ma," I'd ask, "if the bra squishes down the top half and the girdle squishes down the bottom half, where does the fat go?"

"The fat comes out the armpits," she explained.

The first patent for a "breast supporter" was issued in 1863 to Luman L. Chapman, a New Jersey corsetièr whose innovative design called for "breast puffs" to help ease the painful friction caused by the traditional corset. According to the researchers Jane Farrell-Beck and Colleen Gau, who wrote *Uplift: The Bra in America,* the notion of supporting the breasts by lifting them from above rather than pushing them from below, as the corset did, is attributed to "forward-thinking physicians and thoughtful lay women" who observed that corsets "constricted the torso, thereby weakening the muscles, compressing the lungs, and interfering with digestion and childbearing." Foes of the corset argued, the authors say, "for suspending the weight of the breasts . . . from the shoulders, a considerable feat given that the skirts of mid-nineteenth-century dresses weighed as much as thirty-two pounds [which the shoulders were already bearing]."

The long, often poetic array of bra names since that time reflects prevailing fashions as well as women's status and hopes. Here's a sampling: Accentuate, Beautee-fit, Breathinbra, Champion, Fancee Free, Formaster, Hollywood Youth, La Tosca, Lovable, Mardibra, Masterbilt, Nature's Rival, Scandele, Très Sécrète, Venus, Wonderbra, and Wings. The names were conjured to evoke glamour, sexual power, competence, or clinical comfort. Any manufacturer stuck for a bra name could always take the easy way out and call it something, anything, in French. The time for this has probably passed, but it wouldn't surprise me if in the forties and fifties women actually coveted a bra named La Vache.

When it comes to lingerie we owe a huge debt to the French, and not just for giving us the word itself. There is nothing like the sumptuous embrace of Paris lingerie shops, with their individually packaged panties and bras poised on padded, sachet-kissed hangers, with which you wouldn't mind curling up for a nap. If the bra fits, you are in for a chorus of "Oooooh, c'est trés jolie!" from women dressed in that understated cashmere-and-pearls Parisian way that makes you want to go home and toss all your clothes in the trash.

But the everyday bra as we know it was brought to us not by an icon of Parisian elegance. The prototype for today's bra was inspired by a proletarian seamstress who cared not just about lifting and separating but about value, ease, and comfort. If there are heroes in the bra story, the one I choose is Ida Rosenthal, the Russian immigrant and brassiere tycoon whose hand-sewn bras were the seeds that blossomed into Maidenform. Born in 1886 near Minsk, this woman (who probably shared a sizable number of genes with my own grandmother) came to America at age eighteen, bearing socialist-feminist ideals and a way with a sewing machine. When she married William Rosenthal at twenty, Ida bought a Singer sewing machine on the installment plan and began stitching custom frocks. But the buxom Ida, bless her, was appalled by the Jazz Age fashion of tightly wrapping one's breasts in bandeaux to flatten them. Why try to defy nature? she probably wondered. After opening a dress shop, Ida and her partner, Enid Bisset, fitted their dress customers with built-in bandeaux with cups that separated and supported the breasts. Word spread that thanks to this innovation the dresses were, unbelievably, comfortable as well as stylish. Ida and Enid's clients began asking to buy the breast-supporting garment separately. Soon the partners stopped making dresses to devote their business to this new and welcome undergarment. In 1928 they sold 500,000 of the bandeaux. By 1930 the newly christened Maidenform products were being sold at department stores, and the company was able to survive the Depression.

As Anne Hollander explained, if you fast-forwarded images of the American bosom over the twentieth century, you would see low, flattened breasts gradually rise and thrust outward. The single-domed bosom gave birth to separate but equal twin spheres, lifted by the latest engineering know-how to remain more or less on a plane with the shoulder blades, even after childbirth and deep into middle age. Rosenthal's invention was born of a new ideal for the female body, said Hollander. Essentially, this modern woman engaged in sports, went to work, and grew busy with a variety of obligations and diversions that would have been really unpleasant and difficult if she were under perpetual assault by her own underwear.

I reached puberty in the height of the Maidenform bra "dream" campaign. These advertisements were oddly captivating: a shirtless woman in a Maidenform bra insinuating herself, Zelig-like, into a scene of great import. There she was, in her Maidenform, sitting on the UN Security Council or flying a plane. On whom was the joke? I suppose the point was that a well-fitting bra frees a woman to do what needs to be done. On the other hand, as if to ensure that no one take such musings seriously, the dream has her accomplishing these noteworthy feats in her underwear.

My mother told me the Yiddish expression for bra was "shtoppen zee floppen." I loved the joke and have never abandoned it. The funniest real name for a bra is the Dutch *bustehouder*. Italian women wear a *reggiseno*; the Spanish slip into a *sujetador*. Germans don the formidable-sounding *Büstenhalter*. And in France, one can purchase *un très beau soutien-gorge*. Apparently bras come not just in nationalities but also religions. I learned this recently from my friend Norris, who sent me an explanation of the four denominations of bra. The Catholic bra supports the masses. The Salvation Army bra lifts the fallen. The Presbyterian bra keeps boobs staunch and upright, and the Baptist variety makes mountains out of molehills.

The fact that I went so many years not knowing my true bra size isn't at all unusual. You'd think that, with all the major women's magazines running at least one "Does Your Bra Fit?" story a year, we'd get the message. And yet, with foolish optimism, we grab a lacy wisp of a thing that isn't likely to extend over our nipples, or fall for nifty-looking sports bras sized S, M, or L. I remember Erma Bombeck's wonderful remark about the proposed Equal Rights Amendment: "Words have never been so misunderstood since one-size-fits-all." But nearly all the women I know admit that they decided on their own what size they wear and, having decided, they stick to it. The recurring magazine and newspaper features, which seem to linger in overset limbo, waiting for a slow news day, spit out this estimate: 70 percent of all women wear the wrong bra size. For all we know, the figure may have been extrapolated from a sample as small as my polling of my friends. Yet it is undeniable that, while we obsess over the nuances of our hairstyles and earnestly try to avoid having gunked-up mascara or the unfortunate condition known as camel toe, which occurs when your slacks cut into your crotch, we are slow to correct the unattractive results of an ill-fitting bra. The four leading bra blunders, according to Fayreform "bra-ologist" Emma Chapman, are bulging busts (cup size too small), wrinkled cups (cup size too big), bra riding up (wrong back size), and bra digging in (improperly adjusted straps or badly fitting underwire). Why we need a bra-ologist to point out these symptoms is a mystery, since these complications are the intuitive, logical results of jamming something too big into something too small, or vice versa.

But how are we supposed to know what size we are without spending an eternity in a stuffy dressing room, extracting each bra from the toothed jaws of its hanger, rearranging security tags and adjusting straps? Who among even the most determined women can be expected to linger in that room, under lighting engineered for the sole purpose of turning exposed skin into a jaundiced blotch-scape? Well, we could measure ourselves, I suppose. It's not difficult. You take your ruler tape and note your chest width both across the breasts and around the rib cage directly below them. Then you consult your nifty Imperial System sizing chart. My under-bust measure is 27, which gives me a band size of 32. Over the nipples I measure 38 inches, which makes me a DDD cup. Simple, yes?

I know of absolutely no one who has done this.

Being fitted for a bra, insists Emma Chapman, "could be a life-changing experience—and it's free." Chapman reminds us that, no matter how much we run, spin, crunch, or do our Vinyasa practice, our boobs are made of fat, ligaments, and skin, not muscle. Do not, warns Chapman, wear a smaller cup size to get more cleavage or to look smaller. "It will cause bulge and breast damage," she says. She also cautions against tightening bra straps for "more perk." Until I began wearing bras that actually fit, this was my biggest blunder. I had what I assumed were permanent grooves in my shoulders. My breasts weigh close to six pounds; I'd been hoisting a sack of potatoes with sewing thread. When bras don't provide enough support in a pair of melons like mine, the weight stretches the Cooper's ligaments, producing droop.

When I was growing up, getting fitted for a bra seemed like a matronly, even a grandmatronly, thing to do. It was for ladies like my aunts Bertha, Fanny, Tessie, Lizzie, Dottie, and Rose, sisters who all had breasts of Himalayan heft and proportions and who shopped for bras on New York's Lower East Side. My mother dragged us kids along with her a few times to one of these establishments, on Orchard Street. Never had I seen such a vast offering of the world's ugliest underwear. Control-paneled panties hung like the wilted flags of a surrendering army. The bras had cups stiff as nose cones and straps wide as runways. When I was little, an elderly aunt's boobs terrified me. They were huge, of course, but not in the usual way. What made me squeamish was the sheer vastness of their surface area, and the way one thrust eastward, the other westward. I feared those boobs in the same way I feared the cresting waves at Jones Beach. But what freaked me out even more was the sight of her bra hanging in the bathroom. It looked as if it might come to life and wrap itself around my throat.

It occurred to me not long ago that, grateful as I was to companies such as Wacoal and purveyors such as Neiman Marcus for making bras in my size, a bra that fits and a bra that's sexy need not be mutually exclusive. I'd been following links on the Web to bra purveyors offering, in my freak size, bras that were really gorgeous. And really expensive. So I indulged in the perverse reasoning and fantasy number-crunching that convinces us we "deserve" a $400 Betsey Johnson hobo bag, a pair of $250 Masai Barefoot Technology shoes, blinding ourselves to the irony that a hobo or Serengeti nomad might not see that kind of money all at once in a lifetime. I adore my pricey Petite Coquette appliquéd crimson push-up bra, but it is not the perfect bra. It fits well but not optimally, it itches a little, and I wouldn't want to wear it, say, horseback riding. To get the perfect bra, I knew what I had to do. I had to go to the Town Shop.

The Town Shop has occupied a strategic piece of Upper West Side real estate since 1888. I'd noted its presence over the years on my pilgrimages to Zabar's specialty foods—home of the world's most delicious whitefish—and the incomparable H&H Bagels. But I always assumed the Town Shop was for old ladies, women with the lingerie needs of my grandmothers. This changed one morning in the gym locker room after a hot-yoga class, when I noticed that my friend Amy, a woman in her thirties with off-the-charts boobs, was wearing a really pretty bra that cradled and contained those boobs so neatly I was transfixed. I suppose this is how certain people feel when they gaze upon a Porsche. Amy met my gaze, then stared at my own equipment with a mixture of pity and disgust. "That bra won't do," she said. "The Town Shop. Go to the Town Shop, and they'll fix you up, and you won't have *those*." Amy pointed to the two mini-boobs formed by the overflow from what I believed to be my very best bra.

For a time, Amy actually worked at the Town Shop. Since then, she's never purchased a bra anywhere else. The Town Shop's motto, coined by its late proprietress Selma Koch, is "finding the perfect bra is an art, not a science." The Town Shop carries numerous styles and makes of bras from sizes AA to JJ. Other lingerie shops may assuage one's bra lust with temporary potions and soothing elixirs, but the Town Shop is more like the Mayo Clinic. There you get it all: diagnosis, prognosis, and cure.

From its candy-pink awning to the abundance of mature sales help, the Town Shop has a cozy retro feel. A sign posted at the entrance to a long corridor of dressing rooms warns PLEASE . . . NO MEN BEYOND THIS POINT. Yes, this means you, pal—the high roller outfitting his mistress, the hovering husband, the solicitous sugar daddy. The inner sanctum echoes with women's voices in a variety of languages and accented English. I hear French, Russian, Japanese, Spanish, and someone who sounds like my Polish-born grandmother. And I hear the tough-love admonitions of the saleswomen who must break the news to customer after customer that her bra size is not what she thinks it is. "These women are shocked to learn their real bra size," says Fermina, who works the cash register. I was tempted to ask whether she herself was named after a bra.

I am lucky to land a ten-year Town Shop veteran, Bessie Day, a handsome woman of indeterminate age. "I'm a weird size— 32DDD," I tell her. "No such thing as a weird size around here," says Bessie, who wears a denim pantsuit. I submit to her the way I would to a doctor in an examination room. She eyes my breasts and says, "Hmmm." After a pause Bessie meets my gaze and says, "Today, I'm going to show you how to put the bra on so you don't all pop out."

Put the bra on? Is it possible that I got to be half a century old without knowing the correct way to put on a bra? Well, yes. In my pale pink dressing room I remove my bra and await Bessie's return. I will put myself completely in her hands, so to speak. Bessie returns with two bras. "Your right breast is bigger," she says. This is the first I've heard of it. "But that's not bad," she adds. I take one of the bras and begin putting it on in the usual way, jabbing an arm under each strap, when Bessie intervenes, and none too gently. "No, no, no. Just lean forward. Don't do anything yet." I know better than to defy her, so there I am, leaning forward in front of the mirror, my breasts asway in midair. Bessie talks me through the rest. "Guide one breast in the center of the cup." I reflexively reach to yank up the strap, but Bessie gets a firm grip on my arm. "You help the strap up with the other hand," she instructs. "That's it. Help one hand with the other hand. Now the other side." I go slow this time, aiming my left breast into the bull's-eye of the bra cup, easing the strap on with my right hand, as Bessie nods her approval. Then I do the thing I do every morning of my life. I proceed to jam my excess flesh into the bra cups. Bessie groans and grabs my hand away. "You don't stuff it. You smooth it. Like this." She runs her fingers, as assured as a surgeon's, back and forth over the narrow bulge of boob overflow. "Okay, good," she pronounces. "You in. Now put on the sweater." And Bessie disappears.

In my scoop-neck sweater I face my reflection. I look different. I'm . . . I don't know—more compact. I look as if I've suddenly lost weight. Getting into the bra was a bit of a workout, but not that much. I'm seeing a pair of zinger breasts, plump but erect and firm. I take off the sweater and consider. The bra, a pale pink number, passes every test on my cheat sheet. The back band is snug but I can pinch an inch in it. The shoulder straps aren't digging into my skin and I can slip a thumb under each. All of my boob skin is contained within the bra cups. And the center is actually resting on my chest wall. It's exhilarating but I also find myself thinking, What a fool I've been. I have waited far, far too long for this moment.

Wow, I say to Bessie when she returns. "It's beautiful!" I strip and go for the next bra, a mauve lacy number, and notice the tag says 32G. *Am I a 32G?* I'm stunned. "No big deal," says Bessie. "We get H's in here all the time." "Was the first bra a 32G?" "Yes, ma'am. Now let me see you put this one on." I bend down, slowly guide one boob in, help one hand with the other, and I'm thinking, This new choreography is giving me a headache, it takes so long, and it's so acutely unsexy. I find myself guiding the other breast into the bra cup as if I'm double-bagging a sack of particularly odious garbage. I'm making a face, when suddenly Bessie, the grown-up in the room, snaps, "C'mon! Speed it up! You gotta go to work!" She sighs. Then, "Okay now, smooth. Smooth. Good. You in. Now put on the sweater." And off she goes.

There are no price tags on these bras. Bessie gives me the feeling it would be churlish to ask, as if, in the midst of some life-saving procedure, I asked the doctor, So how much is this going to set me back? I will pay whatever it costs. *Because of comfortable.*

Bessie cut her retail teeth at Lane Bryant, where she worked for "many, many" years before her Manhattan store closed. She is a consummate saleswoman in the old mode, the kind I grew accustomed to as a child when we went on family shopping trips. These salespeople made you feel as if you were the only customer in the world, and if something was well made and looked nice on you, you'd be an idiot not to buy it.

The next bra is black with gold embroidery, and I mumble something about feeling too old to wear it. "Put your birth certificate in the drawer and don't say another word about it," Bessie says. "That's what I do." She adds that this particular bra is "much too pretty to leave."

I choose two bras. The total comes to nearly $250. One bra, the black one, is, I'm convinced, the perfect bra. The pink one is pretty damn close. I figure if I alternate between them for the rest of my life, with the exception of donning the Petite Coquette bra for special occassions, I will have gotten my money's worth.

The Tit Man's Tit Man

I USED TO AMUSE myself by trying to imagine the editorial meetings at magazines like *Busty Beauties* and *Juggs*. They're not the *Economist*, but I assume it's a challenge to have to come up with material, month after month, for features like "Mammary Lane" and "Tits News to Me." Even titty magazines need a timely hook for their features, such as they are. Planning for the July issue, for example, might send editors on the trail of a particularly stacked patriot; with December approaching, it's time to scout out material for a look back at the year in boobs. Whose boobs are in, whose out? Whose exploded on a transcontinental flight? In my make-believe scenario I'd assign dialogue to a staff wearily batting around story ideas in a musty conference room. "How about a piece about that blind woman who rode a unicycle to the North Pole?" "Hmmm . . . interesting. How are her tits?"

Do titty magazines compete with each other? "Hey guys, we have a big problem. Have you seen this month's issue of *Hard Nipple Hotties*? They ran a feature about tit fucking, and it's a lot like the one we have slotted for the Valentine's issue. They even have a box of tit-fucking tips. Do you think we should pull it?"

Clearly, no one's handing out Nieman Fellowships to this bunch. But they continue to thrive, even with freebie porn erupting all over the Internet, and with advertising that rarely rises above the level of "Enlarge your penis!" or "Lola wants you for her luv slave." *Juggs* may be the gray lady of titty magazines, and it's a cut above the others in my opinion. The reason? For one thing, it is edited by a woman, albeit one who refuses to be interviewed. For another, those cover girls' tits are real. Flipping the pages of *Juggs* I see pair after pair that look remarkably like . . . mine! But *Juggs* is just one of many boob-dominated skin magazines. The Florida-based Score Group is boob central, cranking out titty magazines and websites for every imaginable taste, and some that strain the imagination. From "Scoreland" comes the most comprehensive, user-friendly quick tit reference in its online alphabetical Model Directory, XEMCAS.org (X-tra Exuberant Mammarian Copyright At Score), also known as House of Big Tits. Score's even more booby-centric offshoot, *Voluptuous,* has devoted issues to big black tits, big nipples, erect nipples, puffy nipples, long nipples, giant tits, juicy breast baggers, heavy gazongas, Grade A boobery, monster jugs, uniquely delicious areolas, younger boob babes, hardcore boobs, unsurpassed milking boobies, and titty-fuck cumming. So much for "You've seen two, you've seen 'em all." And I suppose that the person who gets to write lines like "Hooked on Boobonics" must leave the office each day feeling pleasantly sated. Does anyone actually subscribe to these magazines?

My friend Toni tells a story of the day she stopped at a Broadway bodega to buy a newspaper. Her five-year-old son and his pal accompanied her. "Ma, can you buy that one for us?" her son asked. The boys had spied a copy of a magazine called *Bottoms Up,* its cover depicting little more than a bare male ass. "Oh no," my friend replied. "That's just for grown-ups." To which her son and his friend exclaimed, "Why would a grown-up want a magazine about *tushies?*"

It was a fair question. A year's subscription to *Juggs* costs $59.95. Upon how many tits can one man gaze before he has seen enough? Is there a point at which the man is content to move on to legs, butts, or models of clipper ships? The answer is no. We all know that to the tit man, every set is the first. A Google search for "big breasts" spits out millions of hits, topped by special-interest sites including awesomebreasts.com, bignaturals, supernipple, bigboobsalert, bigtitfans, titsfarm, hugetit, soft-tits, and bigtithound. I feel confident saying that anything even the most demented minds can conjure up already exists.

My opportunity to probe one of the editorial minds behind the boobs came in the form of an interview with the affable, if jaded, N. Morgen Hagen, creator of the *Hustler* offshoot *Busty Beauties.* In Beverly Hills, ensconced in a suite of offices at the Wilshire Boulevard home of Larry Flynt Publications, Hagen labors as the tit man's tit man. Now managing editor of *Hustler,* Hagen churned out *Busty Beauties*—the "cutting edge breast mag"—for fifteen years and he's still putting the *Hustler* imprint on *Busty Beauties* videos.

I left a voicemail message and he promptly returned my call. "Sure, c'mon out anytime," said a gravelly voice. Though Hagen has a job many men would admit to envying, he sounded painfully bored. "I'd like to talk to you about big boobs," I said. Hagen responded with, approximately, Go ahead, ask me anything. Big boobs are my life and I've seen plenty that could put a guy's eye out. I told him when I planned to be in Los Angeles and he said, Great, call me when you get here. "Just don't come in the morning when I have my hockey game," he said.

Hagen has been in the boob biz for a very long time—long enough, even, to recall when the models' breasts were their own. He's been at Flynt Publications so long he's seen his boss walk. I was looking forward to his perspective.

Balmy weather greets me in L.A. When I call N. Morgen Hagen he sounds stressed but asks me to come by anyway. The stress isn't due to his being on deadline. The problem is that his car is in the shop, and a sad, expensive saga goes along with that.

So I get into my rented Chevy and make my way to the House of Flynt. The mother church of Larry Flynt Publications, Inc. is impossible to miss. If the oval tower weren't imposing enough on its own (would Hustler dare *not* to occupy a tower of some sort?) there's the bronze statue of John Wayne atop a rearing horse. Though it befits the *Hustler* sensibility, the statue is actually a holdover from the building's former owner, Great Western Savings.

I edge my car into a metered space and enter the sanctum of *Hustler* and its many offshoots. I find myself waiting on the edge of a brocade fainting couch in a bordello-style lobby, with "Larry Flynt Publications" framed in swirling gilt filigree. Aside from a lone receptionist, the place is as still as a funeral parlor, with a similar color scheme. I can picture Flynt's carcass many years hence, gold-dipped like a pope's and laid out against the flocked wallpaper.

A few minutes later, N. Morgen Hagen is ejected from a bank of elevators. Shuffling toward me is a droopy, disheveled man who looks as if he's in his sixties, though I soon learn he's only fifty-six. His flushed, heavily lined face is crowned with a Warholesque helmet of white hair. He wears a worn pair of baggy jeans cinched high around his bony frame, as if some emergency has befallen his own jeans and forced him to wear those of someone wider and taller. Perhaps his pants are in the shop, too. "So, you were expecting a short fat bald guy?" Hagen says.

A self-described redneck, Hagen chews tobacco and speaks with a Texas drawl despite having been raised in upper-crust Stony Brook, Long Island. Hagen began working for Flynt as a copy editor back in 1977. *Busty Beauties* burst on the scene in 1988, went monthly a year later, and folded a year ago. But looking at the walls of Hagen's office you'd never know it. *Busty Beauties* contact sheets, more than fifteen years' worth, are still tacked to the door. Signed photos of *Busty* cover girls paper the walls. On a coatrack hang wrinkled black dress pants and a ragged pair of pink panties. I also spot a few Polaroids of a very young woman ministering to a man whose upper half is off camera. "These are interesting," I comment. "Oh, yeah," Hagen says. "We were supposed to take down all the sexually harassing pictures. Orders from above." The order had come a few weeks earlier. This is odd. Isn't a Hustler ban on "sexually harassing photos" like a Sizzler ban on meat?

Why the demise of *Busty Beauties*? "The large-breasted, bodacious niche is shrinking in its appeal," says Hagen. "It goes in cycles." The *Busty Beauties* video arm still thrives, but Hagen, speaking in a conspiratorial grumble, says he suspects *Busty Beauties* also suffered from "funny business" with newsstand sales. He fails to elaborate. But boobs of every kind are "so Freudian" they'll never go out of style, he says.

I gesture to the crowded walls. "Are any of these real?" I ask. Hagen points out a cover model with the stage name "The Real McCoy." He isn't enthusiastic about implants. For one thing, agents send models' photos with the breasts all smooth and airbrushed. But when the models arrive for shoots their boobs often turn out to be scarred, discolored, or puckered; sometimes the nipples are in odd places. "We get models with breasts all sewn up and gooey and they have to be made up for the camera. If I wanted to go bowling, I'd go bowling. These days I prefer flat-chested Asian babes," Hagen tells me. "Your boobs are too big if your husband has to undergo weight training to handle them."

The real work of editing a tit magazine involves coordinating shoots for photo spreads and concocting the cloying puns to go along with them. Hagen is fond of the word "bodacious," which cropped up in about every other *Busty* issue. "Bodacious nymphos naked as the day they were born!" "A multitude of bodacious, bod-baring vixxxens!" For fifteen years Hagen was charged with the task of boobifying the English language, word by word. He gave us "entitty," "fullicious," "baredevil," "brapuffer," and "Raxxx." And each issue must have plunged him into adjective hell. How else to explain multiple appearances of the word "cantilevered"?

I have a question for Hagen but I don't need to ask it. "I slept with most of them," Hagen affirms, his tone as chilly as the stanzas of "My Last Duchess" as he motions to the walls and stacks of magazines. "Here's Rachel. I fell in love with her. She was a college student. Bright girl." Most of the girls came through agents, but occasionally models were plucked from amateur shows and dancing contests. "That's where I met my ex-fiancée, the one who got me for a twenty-five thousand-dollar Chevy Blazer."

Before our visit is over I hear a lot about this Chevy Blazer. Apparently whatever transpired involving this woman and this vehicle is the consuming torment of Hagen's existence. He shows me a picture of his ex-fiancée spread-eagled across a magazine centerfold. "Our relationship went to the shitter after her boob job." He shows me another model posed with corncobs on her nipples. "I love her," he says. "And here's Plenty Up Topp. I dated her when she was just a go-go girl. They're a good group. I had sex with a good number of them."

But as Hagen reminds me, he is, foremost, a journalist. "I like my job. I'm a magazine guy. I'm a pretty hands-on editor. With *Busty* I was a *very* hands-on editor. But no one ever pressed charges, and no one got pregnant as far as I know." Under a variety of pen names, he wrote all the copy for *Busty Beauties*. Each issue is peppered very sparingly with actual copy, including capsule profiles and tit-centric humor and fiction. Consider: "She stepped into the leather gizmo, pulling the harness up over her shapely ass and shrugged into the get-up, her endowments oozing through the straps like twin mounds of colorful confection." Yum!

Hagen's favorite *Busty* pen name was Tex Novo. "Where did you get the name?" I ask. His reply is sheepish. "It was my phone number." By the way, I ask, what does the "N" in N. Morgan stand for? "Nothing," he replies. "The 'N' stands for 'Nothing.'"

Hagen also penned a humor column titled "Udder Nonsense." "I was very proud of that one," he says. It was in "Udder Nonsense" that Hagen let fly with passages like the following: "Mercedes Ashley wasn't blowing a birthday candle during her January '03 sexfest, but the time has now come for a piece of that lay-her cake." As Hagen explains, there are subtle tricks of the trade. For example, Hagen slipped a C-cup or even a B-cup model into each issue. "To break up the monotony," he says. "Also, it made the other models look even bigger." Actually, he adds, "we never got heat for any of the girls that were smaller-breasted. But our readers would get really pissed off if they thought the girls were ugly."

After asking me if I mind, Hagen takes out a packet of chewing tobacco and pops some in his mouth. His long intimacy with boobs has taught him a thing or two. For example, the older a woman gets, the more she needs big boobs. "Some of the models were the thirtyish divorcées. That's where the boobs came in. If you're not *Playboy* pretty you gotta have a gimmick. The prettier they were, the less they needed to pump themselves up."

And how does a guy prepare for a career as a tit man? There was a time, long ago, when Hagen planned to become a novelist. "I wanted to be the Kurt Vonnegut of the seventies." (Wasn't Kurt Vonnegut the Kurt Vonnegut of the seventies? Never mind.) After dropping out of SMU in Dallas, where one assumes he stayed long enough to acquire the drawl, Hagen attended NYU and then Ohio State. "I was an old SDS guy," he tells me. "When a friend blew up a bank I said, 'That's it.' My parents live in Stony Brook. They actually gave me a ride to one of the demonstrations. That's the kind of radical I was."

Hagen's first *Busty* romance was with the reigning Miss Texas 1989. "I didn't have a pen on me when I met her so I told her just to dial Tex Novo."

I'm getting a huge kick out of this. Hagen's self-effacing demeanor offers a hilarious counterpoint to tales of his exploits. And I'm learning that it's not that outrageous for boobs alone to keep a guy busy, and employed, most of his adult life. According to him, those gnarly hands have tweaked many a high-profile nipple, and despite appearances they're still in the game. As for other games, Hagen doesn't look to me like someone who plays on a hockey team. But he does, sadly, look like someone who once broke his back playing hockey. "Yup," he says, "my back was broken by my future best friend."

I'm relieved to hear about the best friend. Until this point Hagen has offered only memories, wistful and bitter, of ghosts of paramours past. "I was married just once, for about six months, to a woman who left me for another woman," he says. "She was a cytotechnician. She did Pap tests." Periodically he returns to the matter of his latest ex and the Chevy Blazer. "My ex-fiancée was on *Jenny Jones,*" he grumbles. "The theme was how she used to scam guys. A twenty-five-thousand-dollar Blazer, that's what she got. That's a lot of lap dances. She took me to the cleaners."

I can't resist asking Hagen if he ever dates normal women. "Well, there is someone here I like. She's a born-again Christian." Well, everything's relative. And Hagen wants me to know he's not a cad. "I'm not a Hump her, jump her. I'm a Hump her, annoy her. And I never sleep with a woman I don't want to marry."

I've been here more than an hour and heard, among many other things, about how Hagen is on deadline. "I'm always on deadline," he says. "I work seventy hours a week." And yet as we sit around chatting his phone rings just once. It's the garage. At one point a young woman comes in with a manuscript, complaining that Hagen has butchered her lead paragraph. He asks my opinion, and after I read both versions I must agree. The piece is about diving for abalone and Hagen had taken his red pen to an elegant passage built on an ironic use of the word "mollusk." "Why would you do that?" I ask. "Her version is so much better." Hagen grumbles and says, "I doubt our readers know what a mollusk is." I can tell he finds this frustrating as well as lamentable. But he capitulates, and the young woman makes a triumphant exit, mollusks intact.

Boob expert though he is, throughout our visit Hagen has made no reference to my own body. Unlike decades of interview subjects before him, including physicians, academics, politicians, and businessmen, he addresses only my face. I find this refreshing and liberating. In contrast to the experience of interviewing a college professor who is waxing theoretical about genetic markers or string theory while giving off the unmistakable musk of a tit man, Hagen and I are actually discussing tits and I sense no such vibes. Unlike his boss, Hagen seems to have acquired, through total immersion, a truly restrained and gentlemanly touch.

It is here, in this stuffy office, under the gaze of a thousand nipples, that I have the idea. Why not, in the interests of aversion therapy, impose several weeks of *Busty Beauty* duty on all young men? It might seem to us that they can never get enough, but perhaps the solution is total immersion, what the shrinks call flooding. Make them live, breathe, gaze upon nothing but huge tits until they're screaming for mercy. "Please! Puhleeeeeeze! Show me a pretty face! Howzabout you put your shirt back on and we just talk? Can I have some peace while I read a Willa Cather novel?"

Oh, who am I kidding? The most likely explanation isn't that Hagen's enlightened. The man is merely exhausted. All I know is we've been in each other's company all morning, and I feel a need to gaze upon something other than tits. A flowering tree, for example. "Well," I say. "You're busy . . ." But Hagen doesn't want me to leave. We chat a bit more and then he says, "If I weren't on deadline, I'd feed you." It's a sweet, old-fashioned way of discussing lunch. But it is time to leave him to his reveries, his intermittent editorial duties, and his gallery of boobs loved and lost. Many of the *Busty* girls have moved on, and Hagen seems to take particular pride in showing me a Christmas card from a former cover model. She's posed demurely with her dentist husband and two children. At heart, N. Morgen Hagen is as squishy as a saline implant.

He escorts me not just to the lobby, but out of the building to my car. "Call or drop in anytime," he says. His sweetness touches a protective nerve in me. I want to say, Come on, hop in the car, and we'll go somewhere for a good wholesome meal and gaze only upon the most mundane of body parts. But Mr. Hagen has work to do.

The "N," he admits at last, stands for "Norman."

In Search of Maxi Mounds

THE WAY I look at it is, no matter what you do with her, when a girl's tits are that big somebody's gonna get hurt."

I was offered this assessment by a six-foot-seven, three-hundred-pound employee of Big Time Protection, a private security firm hired for what was billed as a gathering of the world's most amply endowed exotic dancers. But I'm getting ahead of myself.

I was excited. I was in Las Vegas and so, too, was Maxi Mounds. After nearly a year of exchanging e-mails I would finally meet Maxi in the flesh. The word itself—"flesh"—seems inadequate to describe the cubic footage encased in what were once Maxi's normal breasts. Maxi Mounds carries the 2005 Guinness World Records title of "World's Largest Augmented Breasts," thanks to a briefly practiced, now defunct procedure involving polypropylene string. When I first came across Maxi's website I assumed she was a morph, an alien creation born of a union of avarice and Photoshop. When she responded to my inquiry with some girl talk and a "luv ya," I assumed I was corresponding with some cigar-chomping Internet entrepreneur, maybe the same guy responsible for booby-wood.com. We were both enjoying ourselves, nonetheless.

But after further correspondence I grew more confident that Maxi was real, or at least that 80 percent of her was. I e-mailed her question upon question and she gamely answered them all.

Q. "Do your breasts ever ache?"

A. "No, they don't at all, they're just heavy as hell. I sleep in a stretch type sports bra, it keeps them under control."

Q. "At what age did you begin longing for huge breasts?"

A. "I've wanted them as long as I can remember."

Q. "Do you ever get tired of the attention they attract?"

A. "Sure, I wish sometimes that I could hide them or just take them off for a while. It gets old sometimes so I just stay home, ha ha."

Q. "Did you shorten your name from Moundstein? Never mind."

All suspicions evaporated when I got hold of Maxi's book, a paperback entitled *The Maxi Mounds Guide to the World of Exotic Dancing* (as told to someone named Kama S'expresse). Maxi's wisdom is contained within cloying pink covers reminiscent of one of my childhood Barbie cases. And the slim volume, which in the Amazon rankings slightly edges out the *Guide to Everyday Uzbek,* provides irrefutable proof that Maxi lives. More stubborn skeptics may consult a Houston surgeon named Gerald Johnson.

In her acknowledgments, Maxi cites Dr. Johnson as "the man who made me what I am today." Here is what Maxi is today: a six-foot, hazel-eyed blonde with a twenty-six-inch waist and a bust size of 156MMM, up from a demure 36C. Just how big are Maxi's boobs? Each weighs about twenty pounds. If one of Maxi's boobs were a Thanksgiving turkey, it could feed twelve people. Maxi's breasts are so big, she must wear a custom-made bra at all times and cannot under any circum-stances lie on her stomach. I will offer myself for the purposes of scale. My bra cup, at DDD, or E if I'm in Europe, is eighteen sizes smaller than Maxi's. And *I* give men whiplash. She is the Long Dong Silver of boobs.

Maxi's book lays out a smorgasbord of road diaries, history (one chapter is called "Pre-Historic Erotic Dance"), and tips drawn from experience. "A good club for the customers has to have comfortable chairs for them to sit in. Have munchies available like pretzels or snacks. . . . It's also important to have good, friendly service where the customers don't have to wait forever for a drink."

Maxi grew up on Long Island and then moved to Florida, where she lives now, in West Englewood, with her female part-ner, Mini Mounds. On the basis of their names you might guess they were cartoon mice. Maxi has danced in Spain, Germany, and Greece, and they're wild about her in Tokyo. The Japanese are oddly breast-obsessed. Television crews follow her every-where when she's there, and many of Maxi's Japanese appear-ances involve simply posing with a smile while giggling women queue up for a tentative feel. She told me that in her spare time, what there is of it, she enjoys watching movies, sunbathing, and reading an inspirational author, psychic Sylvia Browne. "I'm a very spiritual person," says Maxi. "I believe in reincar-nation. I pray. I have to say the one thing that is constant in my life is Sylvia Browne. I have read every book she has put out and believe in almost everything she has said. I spread her word to all my fans who are lost and want some kind of guidance or comfort. I believe we are all here for a reason and I love life and I'm going to live mine to the fullest and best I know how."

Maxi makes all her own costumes. What she buys off the rack for everyday wear she finds mostly in men's departments.

To accommodate her beach-ball boobs, she has had to make significant adjustments in the activities of daily living. Among other things, the laws of physics prevent her from executing a full-frontal hug.

Maxi describes dancing as her dream job, and she's not complaining about doing porn videos, either. In the best-selling of these, she cavorts with other sets of beach balls, attached to members of the increasingly incestuous macro-boob sorority, among them Kayla Kupcakes and Crystal Gunns. Maxi has plenty of good friends, a supportive family, a loving companion, and a comfortable home. But dancing is what she loves most. "I'll do this until I can't do it anymore or until they say, 'Damn, she's old, is she ever going to stop dancing?'"

Maxi's predecessors in the Guinness biggest-boob sweepstakes have not been so fortunate. When the former record holder Lolo Ferrari succumbed, at the age of twenty-seven, to a possibly deliberate overdose of sleeping pills, an entry on her website's condolence log quipped, "The bigger they are, the harder they fall." Born Eve Valois in the French town of Clermont-Ferrand, the onetime "Miss Tits Europe" also submitted to surgery on her lips, cheeks, nose, tummy, and eyebrows. Measuring 54G after several breast enhancing procedures, Lolo named herself after *lolos*, the French slang for breasts.

"My mother told me I was ugly and stupid," Lolo once told an interviewer. Her visits to the surgeons began after she met and married Eric Vigne. She was seventeen; he was thirty-nine and saw a gold mine in the confused teenager's willingness to make herself over as the ultimate male fantasy. A succession of surgeries left her breasts taut and desensitized. She and Vigne had to search for a surgeon willing to make her boobs not just huge, but the biggest in existence. A 2000 article in the UK paper the *Guardian* quotes Lolo's husband describing the operation that put her in the record books: "I calculated the volume, the diameter. I drew up the plan and I took them to a guy I know who designs fuselage for the aeronautics industry. [He] made the moulds, and I gave them to a prosthetics maker who produced the empty silicone implants. It took a long, long time to find a surgeon willing to perform the operation. He removed the old implants and replaced them with the new. Each one was filled with two liters of serum. A bit later we increased it to three."

In my opinion, men like this deserve to have their balls replaced by diving weights. But, at least overtly, Lolo shared his ambitions; she later told a French interviewer she wasn't yet satisfied. "I'd like to have even bigger breasts. I can't because there are medical problems—you can't stretch the skin any more."

In my home office hangs a bulletin board filled with pictures that make up my personal boob hall of fame. There's Maxi, Kayla, Chelsea. There's a snapshot of me, looking positively concave, posed between Kayla Kupcakes and Crystal Gunns. In another photo, her diamond-wrapped wrists mussing Lady Godiva hair, Argentine comedienne Sabrina Sabrok shows off her scary implants, which have fused to form a fleshy bridge, a condition surgeons call uniboob. A 42GGG, Sabrok is intent on getting to a 42XXX. But so far she's succeeded only in becoming the poster woman for reputable plastic surgeons' plea that enough is enough. Next to Sabrok is a photo of Lolo Ferrari bare-breasted on a chaise lounge. On her freakish bosom sit random blobs of what I assume, in this context, to be suntan cream. Her breasts look to be at least two inches apart from each other at the cleavage line, and they project in different directions. Though Lolo is attempting a sultry smile, she appears to be in great pain. Her collagen-stuffed lips resemble those of a cartoon fish. Her breasts look swollen, raw, and faintly septic, like twin boils.

In her photos, Maxi doesn't look at all like this. She works out. Though I can't imagine how, and wouldn't want to occupy the neighboring mat, she does yoga. Her skin looks healthy and her body is nicely toned. Her smile seems genuine and she comes across in her writing as someone who laughs a lot. I like her. When she signs her e-mails, "Luv ya," you get the feeling she really luvs ya.

I couldn't wait to meet her. I e-mailed her to let her know I'd be in Vegas for the annual Gentlemen's Club Expo and the Exotic Dancer Fan Fair, which immediately followed. It wasn't just Maxi I was eager to see. I would meet Kayla Kupcakes, Crystal Gunns, Lisa Lipps, maybe even Chelsea Charms, another polypropylene babe—who, Dr. Johnson insists, is even bigger than Maxi. As Chelsea's surgeon, he should know. There is a fan photo on Chelsea's website that's one of the most horrifying things I've ever seen. Imagine a Macy's Thanksgiving Day Parade float of Jessica Rabbit, somehow deflated to actual human dimensions everywhere but the boobs. Chelsea looks bigger than this. If Chelsea Charms wanted to end her life, all she'd need to do is a shoulder stand.

Sponsored by *Exotic Dancer* magazine, the back-to-back 2005 events were held at Mandalay Bay Resort and Casino. I couldn't afford any of the rooms there, which was disappointing but also something of a relief, since it meant I would find myself in classier surroundings than I'd expected. I wouldn't be going all the way to Las Vegas to ogle flesh and silicone in some off-Strip dive along with a collection of creeps in neck chains and cowboy boots. Not that there's anything wrong with that.

I consulted a map of the Strip on the Internet and booked a reasonably priced room at the Tropicana, which seemed to lie diagonally across the Strip from Mandalay Bay. But on the wacky scale of Las Vegas, this meant nothing. When I set out for Mandalay on foot the first morning, it took almost an hour, but I had to make my way along an ersatz medieval moat, negotiate the outsized statuary of a pyramid, solve the riddle of a towering sphinx, and penetrate a seemingly endless faux Indonesian rainforest before I finally spied the distant entrance of Mandalay Bay. Along the way I encountered no living human, though in the fake jungle I nearly collided with a particularly priapic fertility god. Airport security being what it is, I'd decided against bringing my machete, though it would've come in handy here. I endured this trek twice before I discovered the tram, a monorail easily accessed beneath the turrets of the faux medieval castle. A human individual is to Las Vegas what an ant is to a miniature golf course.

Here, in the world's most unrestrained homage to grandiose imposters and all things fake, I was off in search of the world's largest phony breasts. Like everything else on the Strip, boobs the likes of Maxi's are outsized, expensive, lifelike but not quite alive.

The comic Ray Romano observes that in Las Vegas there are no wake-up calls, just go-to-bed-already calls. Like everything in the new Vegas, Mandalay Bay is vast almost beyond comprehension. In addition to a beach, it has its own shark reef. I kept thinking of a joke I once heard about Texas: a tourist has misconstrued directions to the toilet and finds himself in the swimming pool crying, "Don't flush!"

In the resort's many ballrooms and conference centers there were several conventions in progress, all with inscrutable Bond-villain names like "Synergy Hyperlink International." And then, legs throbbing after crossing several international borders, I spied a small sign directing the Gentlemen to a cluster of meeting rooms on the third floor.

I was dying to get a peek at the members-only trade show, then dark, in the South Seas Ballroom. When I got there I found two maintenance workers who said the room was locked. But if I wanted to wangle a way into the show, they suggested, I should sit by those windows—they pointed to a few floating clusters of couches in an impossibly huge carpeted space—where "they" hung out, starting around nine A.M. I described Maxi. Had they seen her? "Oh yes, the big big one!" the woman said, giggling. "She's been here."

Would I really have to search for her? I had confirmed that Maxi was definitely close, most likely within a square-mile radius. Those boobs were bouncing and heaving somewhere in my very midst. But where? Perhaps they were ooh-lah-lahing the patrons crowding the cafés on the fake Rue de la Paix of Paris, Las Vegas. Or maybe they were bobbing past the faux Tavern on the Green, which is just yards away from Greenwich Village in the conveniently compact New York-New York. Or, if I got lucky, Maxi's record holding boobs were toppling frozen Mai Tais at a bar by Mandalay Bay's replica of a white sand beach, and I might find her there.

I did the triathlon in reverse back to the Tropicana, in heat that was now up to 98 and climbing. Back at my room, reach able only after what seemed like a mile-long slalom through the casino and knickknack market to a nether elevator bank, I e-mailed Maxi and once again gave her my room and cell phone numbers. I treated myself to a swim in the Tropicana's tepid adults-only lagoon, which enjoyed a nice view of the Chrysler Building. A person could easily lose her mind in this place. I checked e-mail—not a peep from Maxi. Prepared for another trek, I instead stumbled on the entrance to the express tram to Mandalay Bay. I would become very familiar with this tram, which after that first day's walk seemed miraculous.

Back at the South Seas Ballroom, things had perked up. On the trade show's final day, new arrivals were making their way toward the registration desk, nearly naked dancers in towering fuck-me mules mingled with paunchy, casually dressed men. One of the bigger Big Time employees stood watch at the registration booth. You could have screened an IMAX movie on this man's back. I also noticed more than the usual percentage of men in wheelchairs. What was this about? I'd noticed the same thing at the bondage and fetish wear show in Miami. I mentioned it to a friend, who offered, "Maybe S/M's much more dangerous than we thought." Or perhaps it's like the tradition, in the era of Meyer Lansky, of hiring only deaf-mute towel boys for the Mob steam rooms. Also, absolutely no one at the Expo appeared to have a last name. Picture attending the meeting of a medical society and being handed the business card of a neurosurgeon named only Roy.

But I was probably overestimating the sleaze factor. These were businessmen. The dancers, all one hundred of them, were there because they love what they do. At least, that's what I heard from the feature dancers, who work with agents and can pull in a thousand dollars or more a night. House dancers earn considerably less, but they're driven by the chance of moving up to a feature. When a dancer says, "I'm a feature," it's her way of saying, I'm not an amateur and I don't come cheap.

A gaggle of dancers bided their time at booth selling tickets for the Fan Fair, which, coming on the heels of the annual Expo, struts the real goods, the "girls" themselves. I chatted with a feature who described herself as old. She was twenty-nine. She'd had her boobs done—"Who hasn't in this business?"—but boasted that she hadn't had any work done on her face.

Somewhere in these parts, on this very day, lurked Maxi and

her ilk, not to mention the exotic dancers hovering behind and around the Fan Fair registration booth—all showing off the boobs, the ultra-miniskirts, the legs, the two-story shoes. To a tableau of cold stares, I introduced myself. I asked about Maxi, and the girls groaned in unison. "That's just ridiculous, if you ask me," one said. The verdict: It's freakish, it's ugly, it gets in the way of dancing. "A girl's implants shouldn't be bigger than DD." "I'm a DDD," I piped up, hoping to spark some girl-bonding. "No way," said one. "Turn sideways. No way." I guess I wasn't wearing the right undergarments.

The dish returned to Maxi. "She's ridiculous!" another dancer chimed in. "Have you seen her?" I asked hopefully. "Hey, I'm not her babysitter," the dancer said. This was my first hint that the mega-boob acts are held in contempt by many in the industry. According to these dancers, there are only two agents who will touch the big girls. Well, others might touch them. But they won't represent them. Not that this bunch, who seemed to flash smiles only for those in the act of extracting the $129 Fan Fair admission price from their wallets, had much positive to say about anything. The women at the welcome booth seemed to want to be somewhere—anywhere—else. One wore a T-shirt reading "PWO," translated below as "Pussy World Order." I assumed they were not relishing the thought of a charter bus full of grabby male fans that was barreling toward them from LA as we spoke.

Even though—or possibly because—the women were strippers and porn actresses, it was hard to get a good boob conversation going. These women were already lousy with girlfriends. And it seemed inevitable that a woman not in the "industry" would come off as patronizing or annoyingly clueless or both. As for my drab costume, a cropped black cotton tank and an ankle-length sari skirt, it might as well have been a chador.

I'm not used to conventions whose security outdoes that of the Jet Propulsion Laboratory. What gave? Big Time Protection loomed at every juncture. Under the glare of BTP muscle, every paying participant was given a badge, along with a lecture. BADGES WILL NOT UNDER ANY CIRCUMSTANCES BE REPLACED. IF YOU LOSE YOURS, YOU MUST BUY A NEW ONE AT THE FULL REGISTRATION PRICE. YOU MUST NOT GIVE YOUR BADGE TO ANYONE ELSE. Everyone was talking about the badges. Where's yours? Where's his? There's an all-points bulletin out for a badge that escaped without payment and must be intercepted. The behavior of some of those in charge seemed downright paranoid. Was I missing something here? Was Pat Robertson on his way over with a lightning bolt? Were all "Gentlemen's" clubs as mobbed up as the Bada Bing?

My ever-so-sweet request to take a peek at the badge holders–only trade show branded me. At least three of the wayward Miami Dolphins were keeping an eye on me. If I'd hoped that some chaste flirtation with club owners might get me just a look, I was at the wrong convention. While I probably could have charmed the pants—and badges—off the pocket-protector crowd over at the North Convention Center, these were tough customers. Tired, jaded customers. In the vicinity of the South Seas Ballroom, my boobs were mere pimples. "Be off," I imagined this crew admonishing me. "Yours have no power here."

But where was Maxi? Surely she would have been enthusiastic about our finally meeting. I wondered if she would give me a lateral hug and sweep me into the exhibition hall. If I were in Maxi's shadow, who the hell would be looking at me?

The day wore on with more girls, more G-strings, more boobs—most of them incredibly huge—but no Maxi. How could I have missed her? Had she been somehow just behind me, surfacing in my wake like the Loch Ness monster every time I happened to head to the ladies' room or go for coffee? A few hours passed. I began to feel groggy. All these tits and asses were blending together. One of maybe three women there who were not strippers, I felt like a member of a drab third gender, a sexless race of scribes. To get my blood flowing, I hotfooted it the mile to the hotel lobby Starbucks for a cappuccino. The rapt look I got from a businessman fiddling with his cell phone there reassured me in a perverse way that my boobs still carried some weight out in the real world. On the way back to the Expo I passed a gaggle of Buddhist monks and wondered, this being Las Vegas, whether Mandalay Bay would go so far as to dress waiters or bellhops this way.

Back at the Expo, I plunked myself down on an armchair across from a high roller in Italian shoes. He told me about his "several" Vegas clubs—he declined to be more specific—while talking on his cell phone, trying to buy a building in New York City. He said he didn't hire Maxi and thought her boobs were repulsive. Only one agent would work with the big girls, he told me; they were novelty acts, like circus freaks, and they were going out of fashion. "She was here, by the way," he said. "For pictures. Haven't you seen her yet?"

So I had missed her. Well the afternoon was young and there was always tomorrow, the start of the Fan Fair. I sidled over to the sign-up desk, where I made friends with the head security guy and the Fan Fair's director.

"Can you help me find Maxi?"

"Oh, you'll see her. Oh yeah. You can't miss her. She's impossible to miss." For my $129 I received not a badge, but a sparkly gold hospital bracelet . . . and a lecture. IF YOU RE-MOVE THIS BRACELET, YOU MUST BUY A NEW ONE AT FULL ADMISSION PRICE. YOU MAY SWIM AND

SHOWER WITH IT. IT CANNOT BE REMOVED EXCEPT
BY CUTTING. This was a really strange bunch. I hung around
on full Maxi alert, introducing myself around. The club owners seemed bored. One allowed me to engage him in laconic
conversation. As we talked he burrowed an index finger into
his ear, from which he extracted something; this he examined
and flicked away before plunging the finger in again. "Breasts
like Maxi's are not attractive from a man's point of view," Mr.
Earpicker told me. "Besides, I wouldn't classify what she has as
breasts. I'd classify them as Volkswagens."

As for the main attraction, the dancers, they also had an air
of exasperation. I had the feeling the event hadn't been planned
so well. I caught the tram back to the castle, which led to the
moat, which led to the bridge, which led to the Tropicana. As I
crossed the bridge, weaving through clumps of tourists posing
for snapshots, the sky briefly darkened. Could it be? I wondered. The day was cloudless. Only one thing—well, two
things—could cast such a pall. Maxi's boobs! I envisioned
them advancing Godzilla-like along the Strip. I recalled the giant breast in Woody Allen's *Everything You Always Wanted to
Know About Sex,* and an observer's warning that "they usually
travel in pairs!!"

I was losing my mind. When I recovered, it occurred to me
that I hadn't eaten all day. The scene at the Gentlemen's Club
Expo had, frankly, destroyed my appetite. Or maybe the cul-
prit was the prospect of the nine-mile hike to the nearest food
source. I went to NY-NY for dinner because, pathetic as this is,
I felt somewhat at home there. Sitting at an "outdoor" café on
"Bleecker Street," I decided to call my mother. "I'm on
Bleecker looking at Central Park," I told her. "Well, if you ask
me," Mom replied, "Bleecker was always too far downtown
anyway." Later I learned that, while I was eating pork carnitas,

Maxi had made an appearance. And when I got to Mandalay Bay the next morning, there were more reports of a sighting. "Yup, she was here. You'll see her today. All the girls are supposed to be here. You won't be able to miss her."

By this time I'd e-mailed Maxi three times. I wasn't leaving until the next morning and I planned to either participate in or lurk near the Fan Fair events of the day for as long as it took. I arrived early this time, cappuccino in hand, and waited. The "girls" streamed in. Most were in costume, either for the exotic dance competition or to pose with fans. A blonde woman with really gigantic boobs appeared. "Is that Maxi?" I blurted out to no one in particular. "No, no. You can't miss Maxi. She's tall." Another pair of outsized boobs sailed by, but the woman they were attached to was short with brown hair. Along came a blonde, tall, alarmingly stacked, but, alas, not Maxi. She was Kayla Kupcakes, and she was really nice. I recognized her from a teaser for a girl-girl porn video advertised on Maxi's website. Kayla promised to help me track down Maxi. "Don't worry," Kayla said. "She really should be here by now."

Maxi might not have been there, but in a sense her boobs were. Crystal, Kayla, Chelsea, and Maxi are among only sixty women in America, and quite possibly in the world, who have what their beneficiaries like to call "silly string" implants. Dr. Gerald Johnson, the implants' inventor and sole user, has since abandoned the procedure after failing to get backing from a major implant manufacturer. Besides, said Johnson, "I don't do the big stuff anymore. I've been in this business too long. I did enough of them; now I just want to do the regular implants."

Boobs have been good to Johnson. He used to hold "Grand Teton Days," reduced-fee surgery marathons. His one-day record is an astonishing seventeen surgeries. The proceeds helped him pay for a breast-shaped pool with a nipple-shaped Jacuzzi. With his folksy drawl, string ties, and cowboy boots, Johnson is a hero to the highest-profile dancers on the novelty fringe. It's not that a girl can't get humongous saline or silicone implants if she really wants them—a French manufacturer makes implants that hold 4,000 cubic centimeters—but the potential for complications is equally huge. Johnson looked instead to polypropylene string, a polymer commonly used for surgical sutures. "It doesn't stick to anything, it stays soft, and it doesn't interact with any other materials," he told me.

In the same way that Botox, developed to treat facial tics and spasms, is now widely used cosmetically to ease wrinkles, the string implants constituted a so-called off-label use of surgical polypropylene. Johnson had no qualms about its safety, especially in light of the fact that his own body contains two pieces of the polymer, used to repair an inguinal hernia. "I decided to take polypropylene—usually called Prolene—sterilize it, and make a pocket above the breastbone like we were going to do a breast implant but instead put that in." Though he stopped doing Prolene implants in 2000 and has since turned away women seeking the procedure, Johnson said that in the absence of complications, "these string implants feel more like the real thing than I've ever seen in any other type of breast implant except fat, and I have done breast implants on approximately ten thousand patients since 1972. So I think I know what augmented and unaugmented breasts feel like."

Johnson patented the procedure and was courted for a while by the implant giant Mentor, but interest wasn't that great. Johnson's silly-string clients were all dancers and/or porn stars wanting to trade up from implants that had given them a sedate DDD-cup. Most of them had already had saline or silicone implants with complications, such as the hardening known as capsular contracture, caused when the body responds to implants by forming a tight, sometimes rock-hard shell of scar tissue around them. Other women experienced unsightly shifting of the implants; spooky, off-kilter boobs are easily spotted on a significant number of the come-hither women posing on porn websites. Johnson's patients found him by following links on the Internet or through industry word of mouth. "I had a bunch of girls who were top exotic dance competition winners; they found out about me when I started doing this back in the eighties," Johnson said. "But a few months ago Crystal Storm was here and I wouldn't do hers. The thing about these really big ones is they require lots of nursing," Johnson said. A chuckle followed: pun intended. One odd detail I heard from the dancers is that Prolene-augmented breasts tend to get bigger as the polymer absorbs moisture. Maxi's boobs have grown. So have Chelsea's. These women's bodies have become a punch line: "Stand back, I don't know how big these things are gonna get."

The thirty-six-year-old Las Vegas–based career stripper Lisa Lipps, a Dr. Johnson alum, got her first boob job at nineteen, two years after she began dancing in Florida clubs. "I still didn't like the way they looked," she told me. "I wasn't blessed with those beautiful perky titties pointing up at the sun all the time. I had the same boobies my mom had," said Lipps, who lost her virginity at twelve and never looked back. Her first boob job cost $1,800. After that, her stripping price went up; she was earning up to $200 a day onstage without having to do lap dances. "At Hooters I'd be lucky to make fifty bucks a day."

"I was really happy. They were saline, but one was capsulated. They tell you to massage them, but I noticed one was getting hard and staying in one spot. And the doctor was like,

'We've gotta break up that scar tissue—I'm going to have to give you a few shots and break up that tissue.' I'll tell you something, that fucking hurt. You could hear this little pop. I said, 'Wait, can't I get a different implant, you can go in and scrape it?' He said, 'I'll charge you eight hundred dollars for new implants,' and I said, 'What's the biggest size we could go?' He said eight hundred and fifty ccs, with a textured implant, and I was like, 'Okay, let's do that.' And he's like, 'Come in day after tomorrow.'"

But the bigger implants were problematic, too. Both capsulated, and the doctor who had done them was being sued for having sex with his patients. Meanwhile Lipps, a tall, sultry blond beauty, was getting more work as a feature dancer and met the producer John Graham, who, as Lipps put it, "started the whole big-boob thing." From Graham, Lipps learned that she could go a whole lot bigger and join the ranks of Tracy Topps and Tiffany Towers. "I was a good DD; I still had room to go and the elasticity of my skin was just great. I saw all these huge, beautiful big busts, and all I could think of was, I don't want these boobs for the industry. I want them for me. I worked out, I was hard as a rock, and I would be this live, walking cartoon character. I kept thinking, I would look so good with these. I was willing to do hardcore, whatever. I was nervous, I was excited, and Graham said, You're a natural. Well, the new implants are something I want for me, I said. He told me, I've paid for a few girls, but they've always fucked me over. But I said, I will never fuck you over in any way, shape, or form. Never. And he looked at me and I guess he could see the sincerity in my eyes. He said, If I do this for you, you will shoot for me, and I'll put you under contract for eighteen months. I'll get you in the magazines, we'll shoot on location. I know you'll do hardcore, but you just can't shoot for any other company.

I said, Okay, not a problem. Two weeks later I was scheduled for surgery with Dr. Johnson."

And so Lisa Lipps joined the ranks of the Prolene babes. She told Dr. Johnson, no hard titties, just nice and soft. Don't over-fill 'em. "I don't want to be three thousand ccs and so frigging hard no one would touch or squeeze them. He did a great job. They're perfect. I'm going to live with these boobs as long as I possibly can," said Lipps, who shares her life with a pack of Pomeranians, Chows, and Rottweilers, six dogs in all. "If I'm eighty and there are no problems, I'll still have them. There are some very smart women out there who have had this done, and some very stupid ones. Everyone says, I want to be the biggest, and I'm going, I want to be the sexiest. That's what's important to me. I got this done to complete myself."

No one knows what Lisa's or Maxi's boobs will look like de-cades from now, but Johnson does not like the thought. "Maxi should probably get them taken out," he remarked. The Pro-lene implants weren't intended to last much longer than a girl's working life. "What I'd probably do is take them out and just let her hang there for a while," he said. "If you take them out and try to reshape her, you'll need to do a lot of cutting. But if you take them out and let them heal, they begin to shrink down smaller and smaller; then you do revisions and get them into better shape. If Maxi ends her career when she's still youthful enough to have elastic tissue—in her late thirties—then, when the implants come out, and if she wears very good bras and keeps them in place, these breasts are really gonna shrink, and end up in good condition."

I ran this by Maxi in an e-mail later on. Like her colleague Lisa Lipps, she plans on keeping her implants. They're her life.

In the vast carpeted limbo outside the South Seas Ballroom, people were gathering for the exotic dancer contest. The more dancers I met, the smaller my boobs felt. I couldn't believe I'd ever thought they were huge. I was introduced to Crystal Gunns, who, aside from her Prolene-packed warheads, is nearly anatomically identical to me, short and curvy. Crystal looks the way I would if I stuffed my bra with two full laundry bags. Maxi is obviously not the only show in town. But Kayla Kupcakes actually took on my cause. "C'mon, honey," she said, leading me by the hand to Crystal. "Can't you give her Maxi's cell phone number?" Kayla asked. Her voice is a kittenish caricature; whatever she says, she sounds as if she's servicing a phone sex client. "It's not," cooed Kayla, "as if she's just a regular fan or something." Crystal frowned. It is Crystal who broke the bad news. "I don't feel comfortable with that. And I doubt you'll see Maxi here today. She doesn't come to these things."

But something was happening. The dancers and their motley collection of fans were filing into the ballroom for the exotic dancing competition. Admission bracelets—gold for girls, black for boys—were examined closely at the door. At this point, I wasn't the only plainclothes female. In fact, each scantily clad dancer appeared to be accompanied by an overweight female escort. Dressed in shabby leisure wear, the men who made up nearly all the paying spectators were mostly on the dusk side of fifty. Middle-aged women claimed many of the front-row seats; as far as I could tell, they were mothers there to watch their daughters compete.

As the dancers popped in and out from a row of makeshift curtained dressing rooms, heavy metal blared and beckoned us toward the stage. The sum total of this sad spectacle—the stage, the seated audience, a roll-away bar—filled maybe one twentieth of an otherwise bare ballroom that could have accommodated the Republican National Convention.

Here and there pairs of boobs bobbed above the crowd. But

when I intercepted them I found they did not belong to Maxi. I sprinted to the hotel business center and checked e-mail one more time: still nothing. Maxi was eluding me. I felt stupid and forlorn. Maxi doesn't care a damn about me. Maxi is not my friend. Mean, mean Maxi.

Back at the ballroom, it was showtime. With the recorded music blasting us to deafness, the contest for *Exotic Dancer* magazine's Pure Gold #1 Dancer title and $1,000 was emceed by a porn star named Exotica. For all intents and purposes, she was naked: her attire comprised pasties, crowning implants that looked as if they were made of granite, and the most microscopic of G-strings. It was this poor woman's job to whip the audience into a frenzy. But as each dancer, introduced only by number, communed with a pole, Exotica's job became an increasingly thankless one. "Oh, oooh, I wanna be that pole!" she meowed. The crowd was oddly distracted. "C'mon, a free T-shirt to the guy who screams the loudest!" A compelling offer, but she couldn't get a rise out of this bunch. One pole dance briskly followed another, with momentary breaks for a roadie to swoop in and wipe the sweat off. I looked around and decided I wasn't the only one who was bored to tears. Things went from bad to worse when a particularly adroit dancer slithered her way to the very top of the pole and got sliced up by its raw edge. She stood there, bloody and distraught, as stagehands ran for first aid. Back in the audience, I heard the dancers complaining that the contest was badly planned and unfair.

I could not take any more of this. I had a fleeting neurotic fear: what if some sudden, apocalyptic natural disaster forced me to spend the final hours of my life with this crowd? I headed to the lobby and plunked myself down on a couch with a small group of people including a dancer and porn actress, her brother, also a porn actor, and half of a California-based heavy metal group called P.H.I.S.T. Wearing a big T-shirt over her dancing costume, the porn actress pronounced the contest unfair and a load of bullshit. I couldn't resist the urge to ask her whether she'd seen Maxi, in response to which she went off on a tirade about how boobs can make a career for someone who is otherwise completely lacking in talent. "I should've gotten bigger implants," she told me, gesturing at her ample breasts. But she dismissed boobs like Maxi's or Chelsea's as "a circus." She asked my advice about how to publish her guide to multiple orgasms. I was too tired to offer any. I excused myself and caught the tram back to the hotel, where I checked e-mail one last time, just in case.

The next morning, while I awaited takeoff on the plane home, my cell phone beeped with a message from Maxi, received at four that morning. "I'm so sorry we missed each other," she said. "It's been nuts. This Japanese film crew was running me around all day and I didn't get your messages until now."

I wasn't mad at Maxi. I understood why she had to court Japanese film crews. It seemed that, though they will never tire of boobs, Americans were tiring of big-boob novelty acts.

When I got home I called Maxi's New Jersey–based agent, Eleanor Bucci. A dancer and stripper for twenty-two years, until her retirement a vague but significant number of years ago, Bucci pines for the days when the girls actually had to dance. "I had ballet training, all that," she said. "In the old days you had to actually entertain. The nightclubs were nice, you got a mixed crowd. There were more props, more costuming. And we stayed totally on the stage. We didn't collect tips and we didn't do lap dances."

Busty girls were rare back then, Bucci said. "The first girl I ever booked was named Chrissie Darling, who had a great big bust, and she worked every week. She was a tiny little thing, a great worker with a great personality. Believe it or not, she was married to a doctor. It was just different then. Today I can count on my hand the number of girls who do shows every week. They do contests, they do props and all that, but when they go to the clubs they just dance around and collect tips in a fancy costume. They're killing the business."

I'd heard something like this in Las Vegas from Bruce, an agent with Wide World Entertainment. He's booked "a hundred different big boobies," from Chelsea Charms to Wendy Whopper, from Rocky Mountains to Lethal Weapons. In their heyday, the busty girls needed little else to recommend them. Profiles like this one, which I found on pornstarinfo.com, are still common: "Birth Date: No Data; Birthplace: No Data; Height: No Data; Weight: No Data; Ethnicity: Caucasian; Hair Color: Brown; Eyes: Blue; Measurements: Huge Tits."

"Everyone's making more money, it's a multibillion-dollar industry," Bruce told me. But the big-boob girls are novelty acts. "They're not drawing on their dancing ability or their beauty. Guys could think they're the grossest thing in the world, but they come to see it — even if it's just once."

Both Bruce and Eleanor Bucci lamented that the prevailing novelty acts are wearing thin. Bruce has booked girls who can smoke cigarettes with their anuses and vaginas, girls who travel with snakes, and "a girl who can shoot darts and pop balloons with her you-know-what." Another of his clients could shoot water twenty feet across the bar. "They call it pussy control," he explained. Dual acts are still a big draw, but the girls don't like to split the profits. Bucci, who with her husband used to own a Jersey club called Frank's Chicken House, has clients who can shoot golf balls and Ping-Pong balls across the room.

She has represented her share of midget acts. But club customers are growing weary of gargantuan implants. "Those girls are still working but they're not as popular as they were, they're not standing room only," Bucci said. "Now they're looking for girls with DDs who are in terrific shape." With the paying customer increasingly jaded by being three mouse clicks away from a girl of his ethnic preference having sex with farm animals, the next novelty act, according to Bucci, has to be a doozy.

So who will follow the Chelseas, Kaylas, and Maxis? Bucci had one idea, a sure winner: "I had a girl who wanted to have an implant on her back but she couldn't find a doctor willing to do it. She even went down to Mexico. She tried to get just one big breast on her back. She had a great body—she would've been a hit, positively." I was speechless. Bucci went on to point out that that was ten years ago. She was fairly certain the back-breast would happen, and soon.

I wished Bucci continued success with her girls, but it was very hard to draw something positive from such an ominous development. All I could hope was that, if this does kick off a broader trend toward triplets, my humble twins might lose most of their shock value.

I'm Doing This for Me

WE LONG FOR what we don't have. My hair was always as straight as a pole, so naturally I spent a regrettable chunk of my teen years attacking it with curling irons and detonating the sulfur stink bombs otherwise known as home permanents. Handed a five-foot-two hourglass body, I stewed with envy over this girl's long legs and that one's narrow hips and swimmer's shoulders. And as my cups began to run over, I fixated on the bony, boyish dimensions of my flat-chested friend Margie. In her tiny T shirts and jeans slung low to reveal a concave tummy and protruding hipbones, she made me feel as if I were constructed of matzo balls. Too often as I was growing up, I'd recall a child's recording of Hans Christian Andersen's "The Ugly Duckling" in which the title creature (who turns out to be a swan) was advised that "zee trouble eez you are zee wrong shep." Accent and all, the line became part of our family lexicon.

I was something of a prodigy when it came to self-loathing. Imagine my shock then, the first time I heard another woman, specifically in reference to my body, say those words we all secretly long to hear: "I hate you." An ample tush and big boobs as objects of desire: at last the tyranny of Twiggy was coming to an end. Despite occasional spates of microchested prepubescent chic, these days huge boobs are everywhere—at the gym, at the office, on television, famously strewn across the pages of the Victoria's Secret catalog. They are implants. We're talking big, bigger, biggest breasts, of dimensions equal to and beyond those bestowed upon me by the luck of the genetic draw. Projecting upward and outward as if each carried its own BOING sign, they ride the buses and the subways, daring you to look elsewhere. They sound their siren call at the beach and poolside, protruding from string bikinis like too-perfect halves of grapefruits and soccer balls. They telescope and point like spy cameras along Wilshire Boulevard. They explode from the withered confines of the most anorexic cover models.

At last count nearly 300,000 women a year were getting breast implants in the United States alone. The telltale grapefruit halves have grown so ubiquitous that stacked high-profile women are considered augmented until proven natural. The model Tyra Banks went so far as to have a sonogram performed on national television to verify that her breasts were real. And still there were skeptics.

It's not just an American phenomenon. Women abroad are keeping plastic surgeons busy, too. While the United States remains the world leader, with about a quarter of the total procedures from the thirty countries polled in an international aesthetic plastic surgery survey, the quest for mega-boobs has also consumed the women of Brazil (the runner-up), followed by Mexico, Australia, France, Germany, Greece, Spain, and Switzerland. Brisbane and the Gold Coast lead the rest of Australia, with a hundred cosmetic surgeries a day, most of them breast implants. In the Czech Republic, a recent survey found that one out of six women was considering plastic surgery, predominantly breast augmentation. A study by a bra manufacturer in the UK, where the number of cosmetic procedures increased by 33 percent in 2005, revealed that British women have grown an average of one cup size in the last five years, and it's not from hormones in the clotted cream. So enamored are the British of breast enhancement surgery that the MediSpa Clinic in Adlington, Cheshire, has begun offering what the *Sun* referred to as a "kwik-tit-fitter"—breast implants done in an hour under local anesthetic, at a cost of around $3,000. "In years to come, the lunchtime boob job will be happening across the industry," boasted the clinic's director. To the consternation of more cautious colleagues, clinic doctors send their sliced and stitched patients on their way after a brief recuperative nap.

Of course, more and more women are also willing, in the absence of medical implications, to have their breasts surgically reduced or lifted and thereby remade more to their taste. But as easy or as quick as these surgeries might become, many adult women stoically accept that we can't have everything we want. There are still women who believe one shouldn't submit to general anesthesia just to look better in a bathing suit. And there remain those women who graciously accept and embrace the dimensions they've been handed.

But, more and more, cosmetic surgery is seen as a quick, if costly, way to improve one's quality of life. "I'm doing this for *me,*" women insist. I deserve this. I'm worth it. In postimplant circles one is fated to hear the word "empowering." Plastic surgeons refer to themselves as, of all things, feminists.

Breast augmentation has sordid, decidedly nonfeminist origins. The first women to attempt to enlarge their breasts by crudely inserting something under the skin were Japanese prostitutes during World War II. Catering to the tastes of American GIs, they subjected themselves to injections of saltwater or goat's milk. Both were rapidly absorbed by the body, and in the meantime many of the women suffered horrid infections. Next they tried paraffin, or wax. This lingered longer than the fluids but left the breasts sore, lumpy, and none too attractive. Undeterred, prostitutes began submitting to subcutaneous shots of industrial-grade silicone, which at the time was available only on the black market.

You'd think this sad chapter of history would have relegated surgical breast augmentation to the back corridors of Ripley's, beside the chastity belt and the rack. But no. American doctors were inspired and energized by these first clumsy attempts and sought to perfect a tidier, more presentable alternative: hence the self-contained silicone implant. By the early 1960s, strippers were already availing themselves of silicone injections. In 1962 two Houston plastic surgeons, Thomas Cronin and Frank Gerow, began inserting bags of silicone gel into women's breasts. In a controversial 1992 ruling, the U.S. Food and Drug Administration banned the use of silicone gel in implants because of safety concerns stirred by reports, many quite compelling, of rupture, leakage, and serious damage to the immune system. All of the surgeons I spoke with who routinely do breast augmentation attribute these complaints to misinformation and mass hysteria, while women believing themselves to be victims of far-reaching malpractice refer to a "silicone holocaust." Except for breast reconstruction after mastectomy, for which silicone gel implants are permitted, most breast augmentations in America today are done using silicone forms filled with saline solution.

Breast augmentation was once just for strippers and the wealthy, but cost alone is no longer a deterrent. Once she tires of throwing money away on creams and pills and gadgets that don't work, once she hears enough of a friend's or relative's proselytizing, a woman with festering boob envy will convince herself that breast augmentation is as urgent as an appendectomy. Then she'll find a way to pay the $3,000 to $6,000 price tag. Though I myself would want to throttle my beloved should he dare to exhibit such "thoughtfulness," cosmetic surgery gift certificates are increasingly popular spousal Christmas presents. Fiscally responsible single women save up for breast augmentation the way other young women save up for cars.

Of course there are women who get implants to correct problems such as breasts that are noticeably different sizes or are otherwise malformed. But most simply want breasts that are bigger, perkier, and self-supporting. So pervasive is the half-grapefruit ideal that a company called Margarita recently came out with a bra designed to bestow "a natural cosmetically enhanced look." Endorsed by an *Extreme Makeover* plastic surgeon, Daniel Man, this oxymoronic bra is called Evolution.

When it comes to breast augmentation as an ideal of the society, we should be worried, says Diane Zuckerman, the president of the National Research Center for Women and Families. She points out to me that even the drawings in department store lingerie ads depict women with implants. Indeed, if you look at a Macy's bra ad in the *New York Times* or the *Washington Post* you'll see two telltale, unnaturally round protrusions defined by capsular contracture. "I noticed that the women in the drawings had two perfectly round balls attached to their chests, with no cleavage lines," Zuckerman says. "Cleavage is a thing of the past. When I was growing up women had cleavage, and if the implants are done right, women should have cleavage lines. But most don't."

With a doctorate in psychology and postdoctoral work in epidemiology, Zuckerman has taught at Harvard and Vassar and has been a congressional adviser. She likes to cite a not-so-sexy statistic: 60,000 women a year have their implants removed. "The plastic surgery people hate me," she says. "A lot of them refused to debate with me. I had one plastic surgeon say to me, in the nicest possible way, You're better looking than I thought. It's always amusing for me when I watch them manipulate their data using self-esteem and quality-of-life scales. I know those scales well. The reason women are doing this by the hundreds of thousands a year is they're bombarded with images of thin women with huge breasts. This combination is not found in nature."

Many eons ago, fresh out of college with a bachelor's degree in biology, I worked as a bookkeeper for a vacuum cleaner company. Don't ask. In my fleeting tenure, I learned a thing or two about the hard sell. Spying on a veteran salesman's pep talk to new recruits, I recall hearing him insist that they could sell an $800 vacuum cleaner to anyone, even the struggling tenants of a trailer park. "You have to get in that door," he said, "and convince the woman of the house that if she doesn't buy one of our vacuum cleaners, she's a pig." Oink.

I've come across breast implant pitches only slightly less crass, and no less persuasive. Under the tagline "It's more *affordable* than you think," the website breastaugusa.com offers breast augmentation financing plans with down payments of 10 to 25 percent. The Physicans Marketing Group, a financing consortium, urges potential patients to withdraw cash from investment accounts, 401k accounts, and life insurance policies, and suggests using payroll advances and tax refunds. A woman who lacks these resources can apply for a patient financing plan that "makes it possible to have your cosmetic procedure today." As a feature titled "Plastic Surgery Financing Tips" puts it, "Your plastic surgeon wears many hats: counselor, cosmetic genius, and now loan officer." When it comes to negotiating loans, the financing tips site says, "A good rapport with your plastic surgeon helps." Who wants a loan officer for a surgeon, or the other way around? Depending on the patient's credit, interest rates can range from 10 percent to 24 percent. Financing scams and shortcuts abound: some websites preapprove women even when no actual person reviews the application; others refuse to disclose annual percentage rates or the fact that they charge the surgeon additional fees.

If you're reluctant to borrow money, you can win the surgery in contests like the *MJ Morning Show*'s "Breast Christmas Ever." Here is Jennifer Lane's winning essay: "I have never felt beautiful. I have never really felt alive. I have gone through the motions, and done the best I can for my family, however, now I finally feel that it's my time to shine. It is finally time to show all of those boys that made fun of me when I was a child, and turned me down when I was an adult, what they were missing."

Or you can beg. In May 2005 a young woman went on eBay to solicit donations to help her "get the D cup breasts I have always dreamed of. Right now I have a small B cup. I can't afford them on my own so I'm asking for your help. . . . I have nothing to offer you except my thank you, and to think of you every time I touch them." For some men, this in itself would be reward enough.

The profoundly desperate have been known to resort to theft and fraud. In Southlake, Texas, forty-year-old Alicia Fruin bilked a friend's charity out of thousands of dollars to treat her nonexistent ovarian cancer. Instead, she spent the money on surgery to have her boobs augmented by two cup sizes.

More and more women are going overseas in search of surgery bargains. These deals give new meaning to the expression cut-rate. Buy one boob, get one free. Popular destinations for silicone gel implants include Argentina, Costa Rica, Thailand, Poland, Albania, and South Africa, where clinics offer "Surgery and Safari" packages. One hopes that the safari precedes the surgery. I know I wouldn't want to bump along in a Land Rover with fresh stitches and my breasts swathed in a pressure bandage. Since you've traveled all that way, a Thai or Albanian clinic is likely to throw in some liposuction or a tummy tuck for another thousand or two.

A tummy tuck sounds nifty. What woman of postchildbearing age wouldn't want one? I suspect there would be far fewer takers if the procedure were called, say, "gross abdominal fat slab excision." This is a serious, radical, risk-laden procedure involving an incision across the entire abdomen. I saw one once on television and sat frozen in horror and disbelief. I should've changed the channel. I have been unable since then to shake the image of the surgeon depositing in a stainless-steel tray what looked like a brisket for ten. Full recovery from a tummy tuck can take a year, and complications abound. Better to shop for some flattering tunics, or just suck it in.

In justifying what they do, surgeons consumed by the big-boob sweepstakes favor the lexicon of empowerment: "I help a woman become the person she longs to be." "I help women feel confident." "My patients have a vastly improved self-image." And so on. And certainly many women I spoke with claimed to be getting implants to please only themselves.

But ask someone with a longer view, such as the retired plastic surgeon Robert Goldwyn, a professor emeritus at Harvard, "Why do women get breast implants?" and he'll answer, "To please men."

Goldwyn says he would not have predicted that so many women would be willing to undergo implant surgery and that surgeons would be so eager to oblige them. "Who would imagine," he asks, "that a time would come when distinguished hospitals like Boston's Beth Israel would have patients there for the sole purpose of getting their breasts enlarged?"

In his twenty-five years as editor of *Plastic and Reconstructive Surgery,* the prestigious journal of the American Society of Plastic Surgeons, Goldwyn has earned a reputation not only as a leading surgeon but also as a scholar of human vanity. As we sit in the sumptuous embrace of his Brookline living room, surrounded by modern art and artifacts collected in a lifetime of world travels, Goldwyn reminisces about his career. As a young physician, he joined Albert Schweitzer in Africa. Back in America, Goldwyn sculpted and healed faces and bodies ravaged by burns, trauma, and cancer. And he did boob jobs, thousands of them. "I thought that after women moved up in the world the demand would go down, but it hasn't," he says. "Toward the end of my practice I felt sorry for these women. They do it to please others, frankly. Let's call a spade a spade. Would I be doing this surgery on a desert island?"

Dr. Kristen Harrison, a media scholar at the University of Illinois, has done considerable research on women and body image and she, too, is unconvinced by the "I'm doing it for me" line. What really burns her—"It's the one thing that drives me crazy," as Harrison puts it—is that when women say they're getting implants only to please themselves, they've gone so far as to internalize the observer's view, or, indeed, what they imagine the observer's view to be. And Harrison is tired of hearing breast augmentation equated with other expressions of vanity, like wearing makeup or having pierced ears. C'mon, she says. We're talking about surgery with potential risks here. And she, like Goldwyn, uses the desert island analogy, but in far cruder terms: "I say to my students, think about this: If you were alone on a desert island would you cut open your chest and put two coconut halves in?" It's a rhetorical question . . . I think.

In the latter part of his career, Goldwyn turned many patients away. Anorexics came pleading for liposuction. Optimistic women with sagging breasts, bulging bellies, four-inch arm flaps, and jodhpur thighs showed up with helpful photos of Hollywood starlets. Some patients who arrived with their boyfriends or husbands let the men do all the talking. Even if he refused the surgery, though, Goldwyn knew that sooner or later all of these women would find someone willing to operate on them. Some doctors want nothing to do with patients who smoke, because smoking slows healing and increases the risk of complications. Most reputable surgeons will advise an obese patient to shed some pounds before surgery. I know another surgeon who admits to quadrupling the price to scare off prospective patients who seem hostile, deranged, or likely to sue. But there will always be someone willing to do the job. Really determined rejects are happy to cross the border to Mexico, or go to another country where medical standards are lower. Anyone who does some cursory Googling can find stark photographs (see awfulplasticsurgery.com) of breast implants gone monstrously awry. Hence, a recent addition to the breast lexicon: frankenboobs.

In a letter to the FDA asking for a permanent ban on silicone implants, the advocacy group Public Citizen declared that since the majority of implant surgeries are not for reconstruction but simply to make women's breasts bigger, they serve no public health need. The letter made the point that the overwhelming "public need" for implants was not a public health need in the traditional sense, but rather a case for the psychological benefit of having more perfect or larger breasts. Public Citizen concluded that it does not accept as a legitimate public health problem, as defined by the Food, Drug, and Cosmetic Act, the "psychological needs of women who seek breast augmentation."

Though most of the testimony at FDA hearings between 2003 and 2005 focused on the reported horrors of silicone—which, as I've said, are unsubstantiated according to many surgeons—a larger debate resounded. Breast augmentation: frivolous indulgence or empowering self-improvement? Discuss. Is a woman's right to have her boobs made bigger akin to her right to accessible birth control? I'm not sure. Since so much of medical intervention these days is not to make us less sick, but more better, where do we draw the line? Would these same pious critics argue against the right to penis enhancement? Would we trust men to make these decisions about their bodies? And if so, who are we to prevent women from making decisions about theirs?

Known for his charming, humorous, and surprisingly candid editorials, Goldwyn is likely, when discussing his trade, to quote Sartre, Nabokov, and his onetime mentor Schweitzer. But he can be refreshingly crude. For example, he explains why he doesn't do the bottom half of sexual reassignment surgery. "I just can't cut off someone's penis," he tells me. Goldwyn says that as a surgeon he tried not to be judgmental, but at times he refused to do implant surgery. "I don't think these women are necessarily neurotic. I ask patients, 'Why do you want this?' If it's for a husband or lover, I won't do it. 'I presume you've seen your wife undressed before you married her. I'd recommend a therapist.'" Goldwyn marvels at how "far out" our culture has become, with its embarrassment of diversions and supposed quick fixes. "You're forty-five or fifty and your breasts start sagging. To fix them was once out of the realm of possibility. Now there's an entire book about the varieties of nipples."

In a 2002 editorial, "Ask and Ye May or May Not Receive," Goldwyn concedes that "modifying normal structures to improve a patient's appearance and self-esteem and to further his or her personal and professional ambitions is what cosmetic surgeons routinely do. We change disliked but normally functioning noses, breasts, faces, eyelids, ears, thighs, abdomens, buttocks . . ." But he goes on to ask himself whether, under certain circumstances, he would refuse to do any of these procedures for a cosmetic patient who is both mentally and physically healthy. "Yes, of course," he writes. "But I admit the decision might arise more from my comfort zone than from the patient's."

Would he do a breast augmentation on a thirty-five-year-old woman, five feet four inches tall, weighing 130 pounds and seeking to go from 34A to 34C? Of course. Would he agree to the surgery if the woman wanted to go up to an F cup? No, says Goldwyn. "I would not feel comfortable producing what I would consider a deformity." What if an eighty-five-year-old widow wanted implants so as to attract a male companion? "I would incline to decline," he says, "realizing that a colleague might disagree."

In the current climate, Goldwyn's views might be considered quaint. It's getting to be a free-for-all out there. Goldwyn retired at the top of his game, he tells me, "like Joe DiMaggio." But maybe in hanging up his scalpel in 2001 he was also spared being an active member of a profession he views as increasingly tarnished. He bristles at what his fellow surgeons, including some of the best ones, will do to attract patients. He knows of doctors who hire models to linger in their waiting rooms. With their perfect bodies and flawless faces, these ringers are coached to give the impression that the surgeon's prowess helped make them that way. Other doctors line the walls with celebrity portraits and let their suggestive if ambiguous presence work its magic. Goldwyn jokes that he had the idea to hang a photograph of President Kennedy on his office wall with no explanation. "Let the patients decide what it means." "When you see hospitals like Harvard advertising these services you know how far it's gone," he says. "And all the things docs will do to drum up business. There's so much hype. Reconstruction is getting overshadowed by aesthetic surgery. There's no end to it. I could've operated on these people seven days a week."

In a 1976 text on breast augmentation and reconstruction, a Dr. S. Gifford concluded, after a psychiatric evaluation of patients undergoing breast augmentation, that many had "unhappy childhoods, experience of loss or maternal deprivation in identification with parents. They tended to make early marriages, in which they played a submissive or frankly masochistic role." He continued, "In these women, the breasts had come to represent something more than sexual attractiveness, because their breasts were their representation of an ideal self, real or imagined. This was an image of themselves as they were at some former time or as they had hoped to be, an ideal self which they had been deprived of or lost through hardship, childbearing or the vicissitudes of life. The operation represented the restitution of this loss, the restoration of an ideal or former self."

Not that these observations, if accurate, stopped surgeons from doing implant surgery. It's no longer fashionable to psychoanalyze or judge women who choose the surgery, though several studies suggest a link between breast augmentation and suicide. One well-publicized Swedish study found that among women who underwent breast augmentation between 1965 and 1993, fifteen committed suicide; in a random sample of the same size, five suicides would have been expected over the same period. It's a narrow study, one of those that examines numbers but not the complicated human beings behind them. And if studies did prove that women with implants are at higher risk of suicide, is that surprising? These are people willing to undergo major surgery to become more likable to themselves, their partners, or both. Among such women, or at least so it seems to me, there are bound to be many who are unhappy and looking for a fix that may prove to be fleeting and shallow. Another Scandinavian study compared women who received breast implants with women having other cosmetic procedures, including breast reduction, and found that those having implants had more psychiatric hospitalizations.

As Goldwyn wrote in a 1991 text, the bottom line is that patients desiring breast augmentation feel inadequate. But most of his patients seem to have been happy with his work. In twenty-seven years as a surgeon, only one patient asked Goldwyn to remove the implants. Her problem was not capsular contracture but religion—"the fear," as Goldwyn put it, "that God would punish her by causing breast cancer for having altered her body."

Are most women happy with their implants? The American Society of Plastic Surgeons consistently offers that 80 to 90 percent of women say they are satisfied with their new boobs. A smattering of small studies support this; in one 1994 study, surgeons at the Washington University School of Medicine in St. Louis reported that out of 112 patients, 88 percent, or 98 women, said the surgery had heightened their self-confidence, and 95 percent said they felt better about themselves after surgery. It appears that women like their implants in spite of complications, which are numerous and common. For example, the FDA reports that among women who've had their implants for three years, 21 percent have experienced wrinkling, 10 percent lost sensation in their nipples, 7 percent had breasts that ended up asymmetrical, 3 percent reported that their implants leaked or deflated, and 10 percent required additional surgery. But all this isn't to say these women are not happy.

How do men feel about implants, after the fact? No studies have been completed yet. How do they feel about fondling something they know to be fake? I've felt breasts augmented with saline implants and they definitely feel, well, not real. They're squishier and they lack the variable consistency of the normal complement of glandular tissue and fat. My friend Natasha (she's a God-given 36F) and I once laughed ourselves to tears trying to imagine reaching into a lover's pants, finding a cucumber there, and being expected to play along and not cry out, "Nice try, but that's a cucumber!"

With so many women going under the knife it's impossible, not to mention unfair, to stereotype who is choosing the procedure. Dr. Goldwyn has operated on corporate CEOs, attorneys, and fellow physicians. Thousands of women serving in the U.S. armed forces have availed themselves of the full reimbursement offered for breast augmentation. A Los Angeles surgeon told me he routinely does boob jobs on policewomen. "We tend to see these women as single, looking to get implants as a way to help attract a husband," says David B. Sawrer, of the University of Pennsylvania Health System's Center for Human Appearance. But the majority of patients are married women in their thirties, employed, with kids, looking to restore the shape and increase the size of their breasts. "Twenty years ago the perception was that the woman must have some form of psychopathology, but the perspective has really changed," says Sawrer. Some might believe that Sawrer's credibility is compromised by his work as a consultant for the embattled silicone implant manufacturer Inamed. But when it comes to probing the reasons women seek out breast augmentation there's not a whole lot of good science around. In whose financial interest would it be to discover, for example, that these women are not in the best psychological shape, and are either unprepared for the likely complications or in denial about them?

When Sawrer was coming out of his graduate training, very few psychologists were doing work on body image. In his research Sawrer focused on sexual functioning and attractiveness. From there it was a short leap to working along with cosmetic surgeons to help answer the question, Who is, psychologically speaking, a good candidate for breast augmentation? "As one of my surgeon colleagues likes to point out, no one *needs* cosmetic surgery," Sawrer says.

Though Sawrer believes there are sane, healthy reasons for wanting breast augmentation, he concedes that some of the women who do it expect nothing less than to have their lives transformed by a new set of boobs. And how about the suicide risk among women who seek perfection but end up instead with freakishly positioned or rock-hard boobs that Victoria's Secret wouldn't touch with a ten-foot pole?

This debate might be interesting, but surgeons don't wish to be detained by it. "Surgeons," as one of my doctor friends puts it, "like to surge." Only observers like Sawrer, whose job it is to probe these women's psyches, concede that some studies indicate women seeking breast implants tend to drink more, smoke more, and be more promiscuous than woman who don't get implants. Who is a good candidate for breast augmentation? "I ask myself, Are her concerns specific and readily visible?" says Sawrer. "Does she have very small or asymmetrical breasts, or breasts that have changed drastically since breast-feeding? The second issue is, What's her motivation? Is she more internally motivated, is this for her own self-esteem, or—and this makes for a less good candidate—[is her aim] to save a marriage or please a partner? And finally, What are her postoperative expectations? Does a woman realize that not everyone's going to notice? Or that some might notice and think less of her? While our society has become more accepting, there are those who will whisper and snicker." And this from a man who is a consultant to an implant manufacturer.

I recently stumbled on a website called implantsout.com, which, predictably, is a litany of complaints about alleged physical horrors and emotional disappointments in the wake of breast augmentation. I found one entry particularly intriguing. Titled: "26 Reasons Why I DID NOT Like My Saline Breast Implants," the entry cataloged every conceivable complaint, and sometimes its opposite, and then some. One wonders: what exactly did this woman expect? #1: "I could feel the implants." #7: "My nipples were too sensitive or not sensitive enough." #12: "Implants lay unnaturally on top of each other when I was lying on my side." #16: "I didn't know, when I got them, that I would probably have to have them replaced in ten years." #19: "I noticed that my breasts were larger than they were made originally." #25: "I had to constantly check to see that my breasts were neatly tucked into my clothing."

But it's entry #26, her final word, which is most telling. The writer herself seems unaware of its poignant irony, following on the heels of her other varied complaints. "People might like me for my 'boobs,'" she writes. "Guys might date me because I have a big chest . . . but I want people to see 'me' and to be taken seriously. Had I thought about this one thing before my surgery, I never would have gotten breast implants."

Molehills to Mountains

Dear Dr. Rey,
May the Baby Jesus be a tender reminder of God's love and continue to grow as the ruler of your heart at Christmas and always.

All my love,

T.A. . . . And thanks for the great tits!

—Christmas card sent by a breast augmentation
patient to surgeon Robert Rey

IF PHYSICAL PERFECTION counts for nothing on the proverbial desert island, one could not venture farther from that island than greater Los Angeles. LA is the breast implant capital of the United States, followed closely by Houston. I don't think it's much of an exaggeration to say that boob jobs are as remarkable in LA as pedicures are in Cleveland. Cozy in my room at Westwood's Century Wilshire Hotel, I flipped through the pages of the *LA Weekly* to find a full-page ad for the New Me Surgical Institute, vowing to "beat any competitor's price" and touting an "early spring special" on breast augmentations, a $2,299 limited offer. A competing ad on the facing page hollers, "NOW IS THE RIGHT TIME!" with a breast augmentation offer at the same price. The Beverly Hills Surgical Institute, with eleven locations from Beverly Hills to Valencia ("We *Know* Beauty!") offers free consultations, evening and Saturday appointments, and the "Lunch Time Facelift as Seen on Oprah."

I was in LA partly at the invitation of the Beverly Hills surgeon Robert Rey, the Brazilian-born "Dr. 90210," whose contributions to the crusade against the A-cup are chronicled weekly on the breathless E! network. A pathologically early person, I found myself with an hour to kill so I set out on foot in search of an espresso. Settling into a corner table at Le Pain Quotidien I glanced around and immediately felt haggard, pale, and fat. This entire zip code seems to exist for the sole purpose of reminding the rest of us just how much money and determination go into looking good. Manicure, pedicure, dermabrasion, Botox, oxygen facial, foil highlights, waxing, spray tanning, Pilates, yoga, Yogilates, Piloga—I'm exhausted just thinking about these. And it doesn't help to remind yourself that despite your deepening furrows, strawlike hair, creeping presbyopia, and dimpled thighs, you're intelligent, funny, and beloved by children and dogs. These women are no slouches, either. They're parents, they're professionals, they're talented and well read, they're active in their synagogues and churches, they're Buddhists who attend seshin. They do all these things and look amazing, too.

Whether the surgery's a tummy tuck, liposuction, or a nose or boob job, there's no judgment made in this zip code. The prevailing sentiment is, If you can afford it, by all means go for it. Many LA surgeons offer specials: get a tummy tuck, they'll throw in a new pair of boobs and some lipo. The attitude is so casual and acceptance so pervasive, a person can forget that this is major surgery we're talking about. You're going to be knocked out, intubated, cut, gouged, sewn, scarred. But, as you will hear again and again and again, it is worth it.

Years ago, on assignment with a women's magazine, I stood beside a well-known Park Avenue surgeon as he performed a facelift, eye job, and liposuction on an already handsome fifty-year-old woman. When he'd finished, the woman lay bruised and pummeled, blood seeping from her wounds. She had sutures along her jaw and hairline and on her eyes were spooky blue protective lenses that made me think of *The Boys from Brazil*. "Gee," I remarked, "she looks a *lot* better."

I told everyone at the time that the experience was, pardon the expression, an eye-opener. It had scared me off cosmetic surgery for life, or so I believed.

That day was more than a decade ago, more than a decade before my stepgranddaughter and her playmate decided, as part of a communal "day of beauty" that was my bright idea, to give me a facial. To head off the usual bickering my granddaughter decided to be democratic. "Okay," she announced, resting her chubby index finger on the ever deepening crease in my forehead. "I get everything on this side of the line."

Who is this buff, scalpel-wielding Robert Rey, he of the tight black surgical scrubs? Modesty cannot be counted among his litany of self-proclaimed virtues. What is one to make of Dr. Rey's website, for starters? Read how "He has published in some of the most prestigious medical and plastic surgery journals in the World [*sic*]. He has not gone unnoticed by his peers. . . . While the term 'Renaissance man' is frequently overused, Dr. Rey is the rare individual to whom this might apply. Author, lecturer, medical broadcaster, actor, artist and martial artist, his ability to focus and excel is noteworthy." Well, we couldn't have said it better ourselves.

Rey is fond of saying that he "went to Harvard." Which he did, for a year of postgraduate training. He never attended Harvard Medical School. I recall my years as a graduate student at an institution just across the Charles River from Harvard. It was really close to Harvard—I mean, I could walk there! I played flute in the Harvard summer band. I took a course at Harvard Extension. I suppose I, too, could claim that I "went" to Harvard.

I would begrudge Dr. Rey neither his outsized ego nor his shameless résumé padding when I came to know, like, and ultimately admire the man. His posturing, which can seem borderline cartoonish, reflects a boyish zeal and unrestrained passion which, later and to my surprise, I concluded were good things, and so refreshing. On television Rey is adorable, a cross between a soap opera heartthrob and a toy action figure. He's a black belt, a member of the Screen Actors Guild, and a devoted family man, whose young children and cute-as-a-button wife are featured in the E! segments. Yet he appears to worship all women (or "girls," as he calls both his patients and employees) and assures them they are beautiful even as he is poised to perform radical surgery to make them considerably more so. I bet he also makes a mean *porco em pau*. Was I ready for Dr. 90210?

Rey had invited me to watch him perform a breast augmentation. We agreed to meet for his first procedure of the day at a Beverly Hills surgical suite, situated diagonally across North Bedford Drive from the office where he does his consultations. Like many plastic surgeons, he rents a suite; this one belongs to an entrepreneurial anesthesiologist who works with several doctors in the area. On this street, if you're not looking where you're going the odds of colliding with a harried plastic surgeon are uncommonly high. But when I arrived, no one knew where Dr. Rey was. As it turned out, the surgery, though scheduled for nine A.M., didn't begin until late that afternoon because of an unexpectedly lengthy breast reduction being done by another surgeon using the operating room. That surgeon was taking his time, I later learned, because the patient happened to be married to one of LA's highest-profile medical malpractice attorneys.

Entering Dr. Rey's waiting room was a bit of a shock. In my years of reporting, I've visited the offices of many plastic surgeons. Without exception the waiting rooms' predominant theme has been restrained Victorian—plush furniture, mauve carpeting, rosy-hued walls adorned sparely with soothing landscapes. If the waiting rooms had fainting couches they'd resemble the ladies' rooms at the Waldorf. They are meant to embrace the patient, to make her feel special and safe.

Dr. Rey's waiting room felt more like a hair salon. The walls are covered end to end with newspaper and magazine articles, along with "after" spreads of nude models, strippers, and porn stars. A model peeks out from the cover of *Tailgate* magazine alongside an explanatory "Dr. Rey Buttocks Augmentation Patient." Here's Dr. Rey in the *National Enquirer* asking, "Do you want to look like J. Lo from behind?" And there, under the heading BREAST AUGMENTATION PATIENT, next to a "before" snap of a lovely black woman with teensy breasts, is an 80-percent-boob skin magazine cover photo with the inscription, "To Dr. Rey, the best plastic surgeon in L.A. . . . Thanks for the 430ccs, Erica." Another happy customer grins from the cover of *Sensational Strippers* magazine. The cover of the February 1995 issue of *Playboy* is signed, "Dr. Rey, thank you so much for making me 380cc kissable! You're the BEST!

Love always, Victoria." A *USA Today* feature about Dr. 90210 bears the headline "Celebrities Are Nipping at Plastic Surgery." A poster for Rey's show depicts a tanned, sumptuous blonde lying prostrate on a pool float. The words "Dr. 90210" superimposed inside her cleavage.

While Rey's office assistant Danielle tried to track him down, she slipped the surgeon's promotional videotape into the waiting room's VCR. Like most of his office assistants, Danielle had had a breast augmentation courtesy of the Man. Thrusting triumphantly from under an inside-out T-shirt, as favored by LA's babes of the moment, her breasts were both copious and firm, and even I couldn't take my eyes off them. In a taped segment of *The Rob Nelson Show*, Rey boasts about one of his patients, a meter reader who now models, thanks to hefty breast implants. "Inner beauty is disappearing in this country," a thoughtful Rey tells his host.

Lucky for him. His practice is now thriving to the point where he turns away 30 percent of the women who seek him out. The video hops to another show, on which Rey appears clad in a skintight silky muscle shirt, pecs, abs, and nipples clearly defined. "I've had plastic surgery," he tells us. "I had my nose done, and let me tell you, it was the best thing I ever did for myself." In a clip from *Dr. 90210*, Rey cradles the tool with which he will do a transumbilical breast augmentation. Rey is one of a growing number of surgeons to have embraced this controversial method, called TUBA, in which the surgeon inserts saline implants by going through the belly button—the body's only natural scar. (TUBA has not been endorsed by the American Society of Plastic Surgeons.) Unfortunately, the tool Rey exhibits as he extols the virtues of TUBA looks like plumbing yanked from under a kitchen sink. Later, Rey told me that although he explains the procedure very carefully, most women opt for traditional surgery instead. "Maybe you shouldn't show them that *thing*," I suggested.

To his wife's continued exasperation, Dr. Rey competes in tae kwon do matches that have left him with broken fingers on several occasions. I was stunned to hear this. The surgeons I've known protect and pamper their hands as if they were the work of Michelangelo. Despite the occasional mishap, Dr. Rey apparently has full confidence in his hands' power to perform. On television and in glossy print, his bravado seduces us into believing in his expertise; would he dare put himself this far out there without the goods to back it up? His ability to transform women's bodies makes him a kind of god. This is true of all plastic surgeons—in fact, of all surgeons. They earn it. I remember when my husband's arm was smashed in a car crash. A surgeon named John Willis put the arm back together, and we spoke of him only in the most exalted tones. One time I realized I'd left my husband Howie this message: "Dr. Willis called. Call Him." As for Dr. Willis, we watched him behold the latest X ray of his handiwork and you could tell it was all he could do to restrain himself from saying, "Damn, I'm good!"

Among a breed not known for its modesty, there's still a line. Rey gleefully crosses it. It's good to be king, and he'll shout it from the rooftops. "Before these women come to me they feel unfeminine and incomplete," he said. "I do a procedure and they just blossom." I think this is one reason Rey manages to be so lovable, if ridiculous. He's enthralled with his work. He's an unabashed tit man. He loves fame, even if it's the cheesiest kind. He is the proverbial pig in shit.

Having no luck locating her boss, Danielle invited me to have a look at his private office. Though of modest size, the room was regally appointed in plush leather and mahogany. It might have been the office of any successful physician had it not been for the assortment of saline implants strewn across the desk like beached jellyfish. Since the legal kibosh was put on silicone implants, which are more lifelike, everyone who's not having a postmastectomy reconstruction—every bikini model, *Playboy* centerfold, porn star, and meter maid—is limited to saline. (Implant manufacturers, backed by surgeons, have appealed to the FDA to reverse the ruling.) Danielle showed me implants ranging in volume from 150 to 800ccs. The 700cc implant is as big as a small loaf of bread and weighs at least a pound. Bigger implants can be special-ordered, and often are. (Most surgeons agree that a reasonable implant size is a C-cup, but it's not unusual for patients to return for an upgrade.) Dr. Rey once inserted 1,500cc implants in a porn star, Danielle said. The typical patient opts for around 350ccs or less, a respectable-D cup. "Like mine," chirped Danielle. "Want to see?" In a flash she lifts her T-shirt to reveal perfect twin orbs, nipples equidistant from circumference at all points. Her boobs looked as if they'd been drafted by a compass. "You can feel them if you like."

Suddenly I found myself feeling up Danielle with one hand and myself with the other. The feel of her breasts wasn't unpleasant, just . . . different. Hers were squishier than mine, with a more uniform consistency, and a bit less springy to the touch. The closest comparison I can make, not surprisingly, is to water balloons. Not that most men seem to care, but I don't think anyone would be fooled. I thanked her and she pulled her T-shirt down. Danielle's boobs may feel weird, but they do hold themselves enviably high. If I ventured out in public wearing that T-shirt and no bra, people would notice my boobs all right, but more with disgust than admiration. And my breasts would hurt.

Danielle welcomed me to her world by filling me in on the state of the art in fake boobdom. The most recent innovation is textured implants, which are less likely, as surgeons put it, to "migrate off the breast meridian." Translated, this means they probably won't end up between the side of your third rib and your armpit. Doctors try to explain to women that they shouldn't opt for huge implants if they're narrow-chested—precisely the mistake the Divine Architect made with me. You need a broad chest to support a pair of 700ccs.

I must have begun to look confused because Danielle sat me down with a stack of loose-leaf folders that promised to help me visualize it all. And there they were, Pandora Peaks of the Voluptuous Vixens, baring her 440ccs. Missy Mink (500cc) clad in nothing but red spiked heels. Miracle Bra model Sophia Arden (600cc). Patients are invited to peruse these before deciding on an implant size. The less squeamish can flip through photos of other surgeons' mistakes alongside shots of these same women after Dr. Rey fixed them up.

This fixing up of other surgeons' mistakes has taken on mythic proportions in the cosmetic surgery field. For some reason, in a field hemorrhaging with superlatives and come-ons, repair work inspires particular confidence. One might compare the phenomenon to one's first visit to a new hairdresser who gingerly lifts a clump of hair as if it were a dead mouse and spits, "Who . . . did . . . *this*?" I even began to suspect that the "before" photos, the botched ones, are generic. I remember my first visit to a chiropractor years ago. Like a zillion other people, I'd been suffering from lower back pain. I didn't have much regard for chiropractors, especially since they seemed to have cultivated an unhealthy, unproductive dependency in my friends, and seemed to venture far beyond their scope to diagnose conditions like wheat allergies. My first visit began with X rays. After a time—too short a time, it seemed—the chiropractor returned to deliver the grim news. With morbid earnestness that put an end to the chance he'd be called back for a second audition, he illuminated the X ray and declared, "I'm amazed you even walked in here." After he directed me to return three times a week indefinitely, it occurred to me that he probably kept on hand a baboon X ray, with which he delivered dire news to every patient.

In most fields of medicine it is considered a breach of etiquette to question the competence of one's peers. Plastic surgeons, on the other hand, appear to do so with alacrity. The photographs of botched surgeries are not for the squeamish. Boobs as asymmetrical as a Picasso rendering. Boobs migrating in opposite directions. Boobs communing with armpits. And, worst of all, the dreaded uniboob, a result of the surgeon perforating the breast pocket, so that the implants merge like cookies placed too close together on the baking sheet. Dr. Rey says nearly half his patients come to him with boob jobs botched by other surgeons. Why do such blunders persist? Some are the result of bad luck, surgical fatigue, or a patient's failure to take postoperative instructions seriously enough. But they also occur because women come to trust and often blindly submit to their surgeons the way they might to an authoritarian parent, or a priest.

When I returned to the waiting room, the promotional tape was still running. Another talking hairdo was frothing over Dr. Rey, leading into a brief video montage of the surgeon's "four cars, gorgeous wife, house in Bel Air, designer clothes . . ." *Designer clothes?* Just then the man himself burst through the door in his signature black scrubs, lugging a huge mounted poster for the new season of *Dr. 90210.* A contingent of industry types filed into the room behind him. They were researching locations for a Disney movie about a plastic surgeon and were under the misguided impression that Dr. Rey's office was typical. Sinking into the couch with a stage sigh, Dr. Rey offered me his hand and apologized profusely. It turned out that, with his early surgery postponed, Rey had spent all morning taping live promo spots for the E! network's new season. Surgery's a snap, he told me. But this promo business—he had recently posed late into the night for E! photographers who wanted shots of him flying through the air—*that* was hard work.

So here he was in the flesh, a young Warren Beatty look-alike with washboard abs, limpid brown eyes, and baby-smooth skin. All my resolve not to be charmed by him was rendered utterly moot by the fact that, okay, I admit it, the man is incredibly cute. He's exuberant bordering on giddy, and the effect is contagious. I couldn't recall the last time I met a doctor, a surgeon no less, who appeared to be having such a rollicking good time.

I followed Dr. Rey across the street to his surgical suite, where he left me to wait while he prepared for surgery. In the waiting room of the suite, which, as I mentioned, Rey shares with other surgeons, was the usual assortment of *People* and *Entertainment Weekly* magazines, but one corner was occupied by a Lucite case of ghoulish-looking antique surgical tools. Whose bright idea was this?

I was busy bonding with two young implant patients and their spouses, siblings, and kids when Dr. Rey shot out of a set of Authorized Personnel doors and summoned me to change into scrubs. The operating room was still occupied, but Rey and his team decided to prep the patient, who'd been waiting all day, before she collapsed of thirst and hunger. A shy twenty-nine-year-old mother of three, Roxana could not have been further from the fake-boob stereotype. In her pink velour warm-up suit she looked slim but shapely, the kind of woman who would certainly be described as having a lovely figure. It wasn't until I saw her naked and prepped for surgery that I realized her breasts were so small as to be imperceptible; if you saw just her chest you'd probably conclude you were looking at a boy.

Dr. Rey is most in his element during the pre-op consultation. It's more like a pep talk: Rey says the kinds of things that must make every patient, in her Valium haze, fall in love with him. "I'm going to be really gentle with you. You're really beautiful. You're just an immensely likable person," he said softly, bending over Roxana and meeting her gaze as if she were the only woman in the world. From my vantage point outside a half-opened curtain, it looked as if you could dub their conversation with the Bing Crosby–Grace Kelly's "True Love" duet and it would be in perfect sync. "You probably have no enemies," he said. She asked whether the 420cc implants she wanted were too big. "I'm a Brazilian working in Beverly Hills," he replied. "There's no such thing as too big. I've picked a higher-profile implant for you so there will be less rippling, You're a tall gal. I don't want your breasts to look like a derriere."

"You must walk around to avoid blood clots, and give three coughs every time you stand up. I had one girl, out of five thousand, who had a blood clot, but they're totally avoidable if you walk," Rey instructed Roxana. "Put frozen peas on your breasts at night, rotating three bags of peas. Eat a high-protein diet. Do not use your arms at all for one week." Rey told me afterward he had a patient who vacuumed the whole house a day after the surgery. She didn't think vacuuming fell into the category of "using your arms."

Rey stood at Roxana's feet and in his honey-dipped voice told her, "I'm going to give you something. You'll love it. It's just like Ecstasy." Oops, maybe not the right approach. Roxana

summoned the strength to prop herself up on the gurney. "I
don't want that," she said. "Don't worry," Rey said. "You
won't get addicted." And then, to me: "I'm liberal with the
drugs. I don't like my girls to be in pain."

Roxana seemed very frightened, so when Dr. Rey left I asked
if she'd like some company. I sat down beside her and she told
her story. "I'm so small, I have nothing. I always have to wear
padded bras. I'm insecure and lack confidence," Roxana said. I
see teenage girls and how they look." Roxana, who grew up
near Pasadena, told me she was always hiding her naked body
from her husband, a strapping man who had held Roxana's
hand tenderly in the waiting room. "He never sees me without
a blouse or a bra. I say, 'Don't look at me.' It was hard for me
to nurse my babies. A relative had her breasts done, and I was
very curious. She showed me so I'd know what to expect for
the healing. She also had the surgery with Dr. Rey. The money
wasn't a hardship for us. If it were, I wouldn't be here. I don't
feel like I'm a full woman. My grandmother and my aunt are
both small like this. I was working as a teacher's aide, and my
husband's in construction, he works for the city of LA. He got
a week off for this. I'm nervous about complications but I have
a high pain threshold. One reason I don't want to go back to
work is that everyone will notice the implants. I've used water
bras, silicone bras. Once my water bra sprang a leak. I told my
sister-in-law about this surgery, also my grandmother. I think
she maybe wished she'd done this too. I'm a very conservative
person. I keep to myself, I don't have close friends."

With the previous patient snoozing in the suite's improvised
recovery room, Dr. Rey motioned for me to join him and his
team in the OR. Three nurses busied themselves with instrument trays while Rey and the anesthesiologist engaged in a
playful bout of tae kwon do. I mentioned to Rey what a lovely

woman I found Roxana to be. "Oh, yes, isn't she?" he replied. "The TV show brings so many women to me that I get to choose my patients. They're all so nice. Some women who come to me are bitter and nasty. I have my girl tell them the surgery will cost thirty-five thousand dollars and that always works; they'll go away. The women who are unhappy before surgery will be unhappy afterwards. And the ones I pick—well, breast implants are just so youthifying. I feel like I have five thousand daughters." And every one of them stacked.

With Roxana now off in general anesthesia la-la land, Dr. Rey's first order of business was to outline her breasts with a Sharpie-like black marker. As I shifted to find an unobtrusive spot, he warned me I shouldn't, under any circumstances, touch anything. He cautioned me that even the tiniest bacteria could invade Roxana's body and "harm it within seconds." "They taught me that at Harvard," he said, for neither the first nor the last time that day. As he injected Roxana's bony chest with numbing medication and adrenaline to contract her blood vessels and slow bleeding, Rey explained to the others that I'd come all the way from the East Coast to be there. There was pleasant chatter about Cape Cod while one nurse scrubbed Roxana's body and another unpacked a set of 450cc high-profile saline implants. "These have a thicker shell than the other ones," Rey said. "Ideally we'd all prefer silicone, because saline implants cause ridges. But two hundred fifty thousand women a year have to live with these rippling implants because of the suit against Dow Corning. I'm giving you a homework assignment while you're in LA," Rey told me. "You must go to a strip joint and check out all the rippling implants."

The nurse handed Rey the implants. "These are good," he said. "These will look more porny."

A nurse pulled a sterile blue sheet over Roxana's head, exposing only her breast area. But before the cutting began there was another matter of business: a moment of prayer. It's part of Rey's surgical routine. "I apologize, Susan, but I only know a Christian prayer," he said. The nurses stopped in their tracks for a moment as Rey bowed his head over Roxana's bare chest. "We pray that this girl will feel fine . . . our lord Jesus Christ . . . Amen."

It was showtime. Rey would be doing an under-the-muscle implant, the type most likely to spare Roxana's mammary glands and breast sensation. She might, after all, decide to have another child, and she hoped to nurse it as she had her other babies. After tracing the underside of one nipple with his scalpel, Rey lifted the small flap he had made—it wasn't more than an inch wide—and began digging away at the breast tissue with something resembling a lug wrench. To stem the bleeding, he alternated the wrench with a cauterizing wand that singed the tissue, sending smoke rising from the wound and filling the room with the tart aroma of burning flesh. The breast looked like an active volcano. This was the hard part, Rey said, the loosening and dividing of the interior muscle. "I have to do this—otherwise every time she lifts her arm her boobs will jump up.

"I like that you have an open mind," Rey told me as he plunged and singed, plunged and singed. "Liberal reporters always mock plastic surgery. Then they sneak in the back door and get a brow lift. You know, Susan, life is a bitch. I tell people, life is full of pain. So what's wrong with a girl feeling a little sexy?" Indeed, Rey, performed breast implant surgery on his own wife. "That's the Puritan roots of this country. It's just a bag of saltwater. Who cares? It's not as if I started this transformation of the human body. And I'll tell you something about these women," Rey went on, as he poked and Roxana's boob smoked. "They marry better, they get better jobs." I said nothing, but in fact I knew of studies showing that in mock job interviews women with large breasts were taken less seriously and were less likely to be hired. For my own job interviews, I've hidden my boobs under roomy blouses and loose-fitting blazers. And I'd also come across an unfortunate Internet survey, the results of which showed that, at least for a sample, women with D-cup breasts were assumed to have lower intelligence than women with A-cups. If one were to extrapolate on this inverse relationship, I must be perceived as a blithering idiot.

Rey paused to inject a brew of painkiller and antiseptic into the open breast. "The darker races heal more poorly," he remaked as he worked. "The white women heal better and faster. But they're the ones who wrinkle at a much younger age."

Rey jammed the uninflated implant into the volcano's cavity and worked it under the flesh evenly. Meanwhile, his assistant measured 450cc of saline into an outsized syringe worthy of a Marx Brothers routine. Everyone in the room counted the ccs aloud and in perfect unison as Rey slowly injected the liquid through a needle into the implant. And, miracle of miracles, Roxana's breast inflated before my eyes. Expanding evenly like a balloon, a boob was born. Where there had been nearly nothing, there was now a plump D-cup breast. Before Rey closed it up he inserted a drainage tube about the width of a drinking straw into the incision. "The tubes will stay in for a few days," he explained. "Doctors don't like to put the drainage tubes in because they cost three hundred dollars and they'd rather take that as profit. But it really cuts down on the bruising. And if you don't drain the breast properly, you get scar tissue and the breast becomes hard."

It wasn't until I witnessed his stitching that I came to appreciate Dr. Rey's gift. Tacky celebrity aside, the man is an artist.

Only moments after he'd sewed up the wound, leaving a tiny opening for the tube, Roxana's new breast looked nearly normal. This was because the incision was so small. "We struggle with a tiny little hole," Rey said. "But anyone, any idiot—a monkey can do surgery through a big slice."

Rey repeated the process—the slicing, the digging, the volcano, and the giant syringe—with the other breast. And then, like a carpenter forced to work without a level, he walked to Roxana's feet and squinted intently over her toes at the new set of breasts. "She's much wider on the left," he said. He proceeded to work the breast like a sculptor molding clay. His used his fingers to press, round, and lift his creations, leaving them "a little higher, because she'll drop for the rest of her—their—lives." This, he said, is the art part. "I work the breasts to make them look real pretty.

"This isn't a business, you know," he said to me. "It's a religion."

The anesthesiologist propped Roxana into a nearly seated position, and Rey wrapped her new breasts in a pressure bandage. Even this he did artfully, so the fully wrapped bandage looked like something from a Jil Sander runway show. By the time I had changed out of my scrubs Roxana was awake, still groggy but, in her mind, a "complete" woman for the first time in her life.

Over the next few weeks Roxana and I spoke on the phone and exchanged e-mails. "They still feel foreign," she told me, two weeks after surgery. "They're kind of firm. When I'm sitting and then I stand, they feel like a contracting muscle. They kind of squeeze. I haven't taken any pain pills since three days after the surgery." When Roxana's healing had progressed she went shopping for blouses. "I felt like now I could try on any blouse, so I chose two," she said. "One shows too much cleavage, I think, and the other has spaghetti straps." Her husband is "very happy," she said. "But I felt kind of embarrassed around my boys and I've been covering my boobs up with sweaters. My daughter, who's nineteen months old, tried to touch them. They've dropped a little since the swelling's gone down. I bought a few 34C sports bras, up from my old size of 34AA. I'm still not used to it. I always covered myself up, I wore lots of black tops." Roxana told me her biggest fear was that she'd roll over in her sleep or do something else to "damage or squash them."

Months later I heard from Roxana again. "Susie, I am feeling great!" she wrote. "I went to visit Dr. Rey's office for my six-month checkup. I was told I healed very nicely and they look great. I was so happy to hear those words. You know Susie, the only thing that I am not satisfied with is that I lost a little bit of the areola where the suture was, and the stitching is not as straight as the other suture. Am I just being too analytic? Well, I have to weigh it out and pretty much end up being very grateful for what my husband paid for.

"One more thing," she wrote. "I feel very comfortable with the implants but I am still very conservative about showing cleavage in public. I feel like it's not very respectful of me. Other than that I have no regrets and I hope these implants last a long time. I have had fears of my implants leaking or popping and even evaporating (ha ha hopefully not)! Much love to you and your family, Your friend, Roxana."

After Roxana's surgery I found Dr. Rey in the waiting room speaking softly to her husband. I went over to say good-bye to them and told Dr. Rey, "Obrigado," which is Portuguese for "Thank you." "Did you hear that?" he said. "Speaking Portuguese to a Brazilian! Details!" Everything, Rey gushed, is in the details. "They taught me that at Harvard."

Sometimes when I'm flipping channels I pause for a bit to watch Dr. Rey in his E! spotlight, gallivanting around the operating room while another set of implants is being readied for their cozy new home. Though his wife seems a bit worse for wear, Dr. Rey is still having the time of his life. On the basis of the show alone, several people have ridiculed him in my company. I see their point: The man's vanity knows no bounds and his hunger for publicity is nothing less than maniacal. His awestruck odes to his "girls" can be hard to swallow. Yet I find myself defending him. He's got a way with a scalpel, he's passionate, and I like him—precisely, I must admit, for all the things they didn't teach him at Harvard.

Pills, Potions, Lotions, and Hope

I WAS A NINE-YEAR-OLD at summer camp when I first observed the freakish spectacle of females flapping their bent arms like dodo birds in an effort to get bigger breasts. I might have concluded that they were, in fact, merely imitating dodo birds had they not been bleating in unison the following: "I *must*, I *must*, I must improve my bust! 'Cause it's *better*, it's *better*, it's better for the sweater!"

"Better for the sweater"? This made no sense to me. In no way did my sweaters, or what was good for them, yet rate among my already long and growing list of things about which to feel self-conscious. But one thing I did know then, if only intuitively, was that these girls' antics would accomplish nothing. Most of them had a few years of growing to do anyway, so their flapping had little, if any, urgency.

As for me, I did nothing to acquire the fleshy orbs that lie beside me through the night, nestled on top of each other and against me like kittens. I've just got 'em, for better and for worse. So I suppose I should feel lucky, given that millions of women have undergone major surgery to get something similar, and millions more pay dearly for pills, creams, massage, and even hypnosis in hopes of enlarging their breasts. How many other physical qualities of mine would people pay a pile of money, much less a dime, to possess? Are women in search of "character" having ethnic bumps like mine implanted in their noses? Are they going under the knife to get their legs shortened?

Given the expense and risks of surgery, it's understandable that women desiring bigger boobs will be seduced by cheaper, far less invasive alternatives. Do any of these pills, potions, gizmos, and other nonsurgical regimens actually work?

I'm amazed that enough women believe in breast enhancement through hypnosis, for example, to make such a promise profitable. I'm reminded of the woman who constantly complains that her breasts are too small. One day her husband suggests she spend about fifteen minutes a day rubbing the space between her boobs with toilet paper. "How is that supposed to do anything?" she asks. And he replies, "It worked for your butt, didn't it?"

Okay, it's a nasty joke, and I don't make a habit of repeating it. I use it here strictly for the purpose of comparison. Some of the pitches I've seen have about as much logic to recommend them as rubbing oneself with toilet paper. Of course it would have to be special ("Act now and get one roll completely free!") "breast enhancement" toilet paper. Dispense with the toilet paper, and that rubbing motion in and of itself might constitute an "ancient technique."

Breast enhancement pitches often cash in on the "ancient" angle. When it comes to fatuous credibility, "ancient" seems to do for "technique" what "Swiss" did to broaden the allure of skin care. I often wonder how "ancient" became such a selling point. Wasn't every "thousand-year-old" remedy conceived in a time when people generally believed the earth was flat and our bodies consisted of "humors," the germ theory was many centuries away, and bras were made out of pewter? For a period of several months I endured acupuncture in hopes of avoiding further surgery for a back problem. My first revelation was, It hurts! Don't let anyone tell you it doesn't. Second, one morning as Arthur, my acupuncturist and good friend, jabbed at the joints of my feet, he spoke of his days as a student of ancient Chinese medicine. And for some reason that word "ancient" hit a nerve. Well, more likely it was the needle he was forcing into my big toe that hit a nerve, but I sprang up and said, "Hey wait a second! This stuff was invented centuries before anyone saw an X ray! What the hell did they know?" Arthur laughed while proceeding to jab me just a wee bit harder.

As I investigated purported methods of enhancing breasts without surgery, I found myself so inured to snake oil that I believe I'm impossible to shock, at least in this department. According to literature for a breast enlargement system called ANBES, breast massage "techniques 7 & 8" make your breasts "centralize and give you the cleavage over a period of time." Then there's Yvonne Lee of enhanceyourbreast.com, whose book includes breast enhancement lunch and dinner menus as well as an "ancient" breast enhancement recipe that doubles as soup and a bath. "It doesn't matter if you use it to make soup, or for spa, or even both," writes Yvonne. "It certainly helps to enhance your breast, basing on the unique properties of the ingredients."

I can't help thinking of the joke about the guy who wishes for a penis down to his knees. You know the one. The sly genie indulges him by shrinking his legs. Then there's the fellow who comes up with a pill that does, in fact, grow hair instantly—on your liver. We're deep in "Be careful what you wish for" territory here. The only thing creepier than these products being useless is the notion they might actually work too well. Think of the ensuing mischief. Rub "Go Bust" on your philandering husband while he sleeps, and in the morning, the ultimate revenge—man-boobs!

Consider the latest boob fad to engulf Japan. Though the Japanese are far less enamored of cosmetic surgery than the Americans and Europeans, the petitely proportioned women of that nation want bigger boobs. They want them so badly they have put a fortune in the hands of the purveyors of something called Bust-Up Gum. The website offers an irresistible pitch for the stuff. "Bust rise gum . . . in order to obtain the bust of yearning." Bust-Up is, we are told in a translation more suited to a tract on metaphysics, "for the woman now, is not is." Each square of Bust-Up Gum delivers, according to the manufacturer, sugar, dextroglucose (also sugar), thick malt syrup, softening agent, perfume, brightener, "sourness charge," "coloration charge," "Arabic gum," and its active herbal ingredient, "chest tree." Each vial bears the warning, "When being thought, it is not agreeable to constitution, please decrease the quantity or stop, consult the doctor."

But when it comes to breast lust, Japanese women have nothing on women of the Americas and Europe. And there is apparently no limit to how lofty the claims for these products can get. An issue of the Bliss catalog, for example, offered something called Bust Booster, a "doctor developed gel" promising to "dramatically increase your cup size in—cross our hearts—less than fifteen minutes." If this is true, then, apart from frantically stuffing your bra with tissues, this is the only way to enhance your breasts in the time it takes for a blind date to wend his way from the lobby to your apartment door.

A four-ounce tub of Bliss's Go Bust (Bust Booster was discontinued) sells for $67. And so, in the name of science, I ordered some and passed it along to my friend Valerie, whose breasts are the size of a pubescent teenager's. Valerie and I were at her studio, about to go out to dinner, and I urged her to put the cream on before we left. She slipped out of her shirt and gave each breast a good coating. I stood back for effect. We waited. We knew it was a joke but couldn't stop ourselves from doing boob checks all through dinner. Valerie used the cream religiously, several times a day for weeks, until she'd scooped out every last drop. Do I really need to mention that she will not be the next Go Bust calendar girl? How many women, at this very moment, are giving their credit card information in exchange for the same useless product?

Bust Booster, Go Bust, and Bust-Up are just a few among the rampant and unregulated gels, creams, pills, and potions that beckon from nearly 240,000 come-hither sites on the Internet. I call them porno-ceuticals, especially since so many of these companies offer the complete package—bigger breasts for you, bigger penis for him. And that's not to mention the pitches for breast-enlarging hypnosis ("You are getting bust-eeeeeee"), self-massage, and vacuum pumps. Hypnotica, a self-hypnosis system marketed by Charles E. Henderson, Ph.D., offers "induction" audiotapes or CDs that guide us to the level of relaxation necessary for the suggestion—in this case, bigger boobs—to take hold. Here's a portion of the script: "As I continue to be deeply relaxed, and to become even more relaxed, I am thinking about my suggestion." (At this point insert your suggestion). "All of the suggestions I have given myself will be effective because they are right for me and it is good that I should achieve them. . . ." Whether you desire bigger boobs or freedom from an addiction, this should do the trick. Who would imagine it could be so simple? And I gather that if you don't like them you can put yourself in a trance and make them go away.

For sheer chutzpah, I was particularly impressed by a method advanced by one Khemmika na Songkhla of Bangkok. According to an account in an online Malaysian newspaper, Khemmika claims she can enlarge breasts by up to six centimeters without laying a hand on the breasts themselves. With her bare palms, Khemmika, thirty-four, slaps the client's torso on the back and abdomen. This, she asserts, "transfers fatty tissue from those parts of the body to the breasts."

Upon reading this I had two thoughts: One, why hasn't anyone else thought of this? It's so simple and clean and, as Khemmika helpfully notes, "not only is the procedure cheaper than plastic surgery, but there is also no pain involved." Two, has anyone investigated the breast-enhancing effects of the Heimlich maneuver? Khemmika charges a mere 16,000 baht, or $380, for six days of ten-minute "treatments," after which results will be obvious. If clients are initially skeptical, Khemmika offers her most convincing pitch. She shows them her own breasts, proving . . . what? Did she slap herself around? "As soon as women see and touch my breasts, they want to have the treatment," says Khemmika, who learned this traditional method from her late grandmother. Actually I think all a person needs to know about the veracity of these claims is right there in the headline: "Slap on back enlarges breasts, says woman." Says you.

One hard-sell tactic that is wearing quite thin is the claim that some breast enhancement product proved highly effective in studies done "in Europe." I know what they're thinking. "Hey, it's okay to just say that. It's not like they'll ever *go* there." I find these claims as convincing as the television commercials touting Europe's torrid love affair with Zamfir. Without hard corroborating evidence I find it impossible to believe that the citizens of Barcelona or Zurich are frantically downloading pan-flute classics onto their MP3 players.

After I e-mailed inquiries about breast-enlarging hypnosis and ordered a complimentary CD on breast-enhancing massage, I suddenly acquired a new best girlfriend named Hilary. With subject headings such as "Why You Should Do Breast Massage" and "Breast Care: A Must for You," e-mails from Hilary began arriving every few days, and they're still coming. The unreadable disk was accompanied by material promising, "By Invitation Only!" "The Astonishing Secrets of the Most Ancient . . . Most Unknown . . . and Most Sought After Breast Enhancement Methods in the World." An alert reader might be tipped off by the oxymoronic "most sought after" yet "most unknown," but Hilary's associate boob expert Yvonne goes on to promise not one, not two, but "30 ways to enhance your breast, at any age."

"Dear friend," Yvonne writes, kicking off an epistle woven with boldface. "With our permission (and with strict precautions for privacy), I am going to send you one of the **most important and exciting books** ever released on 'Breast Enhancement.' News of this surprising 'best-seller' is spreading like wildfire among women in every age group. In it you will find the **complete 'secret' enhancement** that all women desire—including ancient methods used thousands of years ago to important facts on modern day breast enhancement surgery. It is so well covered . . . **even Breast Augmentation Doctors are impressed!**"

Never mind the indemnifying quotation marks ("best-seller," "Breast Enhancement"). After I'd plodded through a festering mulch of superlatives I learned that Yvonne would like to sell me the following: A "miracle woman herb found at an altitude of 300 to 800 metres above sea level." "2 most effective and commonly used essential oils for breast enhancement that you can buy off the rack easily." Yogalike postures that are "being explored and then practice by generations of Tibetan monks."

Well of course, who hasn't suppressed the urge to say "Hubba hubba!" when those monks shuffle by? But how on earth did Yvonne win the glowing endorsements—accompanied by beaming headshots—of reputable plastic surgeons in Longmeadow, Massachusetts; Boca Raton, Florida; and Orange, California? Would they extol as a "valuable resource" a book that includes a breast-enhancement brew that can be imbibed or bathed in?

"I was sent an e-mail by Ms. Lee," one doctor said. "The portions I read seemed reasonable but obviously other portions of the book are not. It seemed like a good and easy way to gain exposure with an audience interested in breast augmentation. It may have been a mistake on my part." Another doctor, in New York City, said his description of the book as "refreshing" and his expression of a desire to buy copies for his patients were based on seeing only a "small portion" of it. All the surgeons were apparently shown sections of Lee's final chapter, which discusses surgical options and what to expect. You've got to admire her cheek for doing the follow-up cut and paste that gives the impression doctors are singing the praises of breast-enhancing soup.

With high-profile supplement producers pulling in tens of millions of dollars, where are all these non–surgically enhanced babes keeping themselves? If any of these methods deliver what they promise, why the stampede for implants? How many women other than Victoria's Secret models and porn stars would bother with implants if a slathering of cream would do the job?

Does *any* of this stuff actually work?

I decided to consult James Duke, the thinking woman's herbalist. The author of *The Green Pharmacy,* Duke is no flake. For decades, at the behest of the U.S. Department of

PILLS, POTIONS, LOTIONS, AND HOPE

Agriculture, the blunt-spoken Colonel Sanders look-alike combed the planet for traditional medicinal herbs and put these to the test in state-of-the-art laboratories. I'm a tough customer, but Duke is the guy who got me drinking pomegranate juice, which I find vile, to ward off the insults of perimenopause. At his home in a suburb of Baltimore, the now retired botanist tends a sprawling herb garden in which sections are labeled for their proven healing qualities. As he walked me through the place, we stopped to gaze at lovely clusters of dozens of herbs including saw palmetto, aloe, and St. John's wort that curled around stones carved somewhat ghoulishly with the words "prostate," "cystitis," and "menopause." For the unsqueamish, Duke offers many tales of feverish adventures and septic close calls in, for example, the jungles of Panama, their happy endings precipitated by the use of the right indigenous herbs.

Duke told me about a concoction of his called Bustea, marketed by Greenbush Natural Products. Here are some sample Greenbush testimonials: "I have been using the breast enlargement herbs since April. I went and got measured at Victoria's Secret and I am a 34B! (Up from 34A.)" "I am following your instructions exactly and in eight days increased my bust one inch."

Though he wanted no part of these breathless pronouncements, Duke explained that Bustea contains ingredients proven to improve the condition known as "micromastia"—small boobs, to you—if the tea is used faithfully. The brew includes fenugreek, anise, caraway, fennel, and lemongrass, all said to increase the size of breasts and promote lactation. Other lactogenic herbs include hops, white mulberry, dill, black cumin, sweetroot, parsley, and star anise. These herbs turn up in pill form in many breast enhancement supplements. One of these, Femenique, promises a blend of these "essential botanicals" along with "hard to find extracts" that deliver results "exponentially" stronger than competing products.

"I think that many of the bust enhancement supplements were patterned after my Bustea," Duke said. "Like most drugs and herbs interacting with the very variable human genome, they work for some genomes but not for others."

I ordered a bag of Bustea and brewed a cup to see what it tasted like. Awful. It is akin to, perhaps, a cocktail of licorice and mothballs. But that is where my self-experimentation ended. Suppose the stuff really works. Considering I had just spent about $500 on bras that actually fit, I didn't want to screw around. I pictured my husband arriving home one day to see nothing but flesh pressed against the windows. After forcing open the door, he is knocked down by a boob expanding as if fed by a high-powered helium pump. Kind of like that pudding mix in the movie *Sleeper*.

That's where my friend Lois came in. Lois despises her small breasts. Years after we'd grown really close, she admitted it was a challenge for her to transcend her jealousy of my huge boobs. She looks fine to me. But Lois is tall and big-boned and has longed her entire adult life for a set of knockers worthy of her statuesque dimensions. I set her up with a sack of Bustea and said, "Drink! Drink like you've never drunk before!" The first few times she nearly gagged on the stuff.

Because they are herbal supplements and not pharmaceuticals, breast enhancement products are not subject to Food and Drug Administration scrutiny for their effectiveness, only for their general safety. In fact, these pills and potions are, for regulatory purposes, in the same category as, say, chamomile tea. Legitimate controlled studies of breast pills are practically nonexistent. That's because such studies are costly, and even if fenugreek and anise are effective breast enhancers they can't be patented. They grow wild in nature, which is the original public domain. It's a lot easier and more profitable to spend money on snazzy, seductive advertising, offer vapid guarantees, and then disappear into the ether if someone complains.

Of course, there is one group willing to invest in studies of breast enhancement supplements, a group that stands to gain a lot by disproving their claims. Late in 2004, *Plastic and Reconstructive Surgery,* the official journal of the American Society of Plastic Surgeons, published a study indicating that these pills are ineffective or potentially dangerous, and some may be both. One product, for example, called Vanity, vows a one-to-two-cup increase in breast size by "fooling your breasts into believing you're pregnant." If the claim is nonsense, you've thrown your money away. If the claim is valid, on the other hand, and the pills really do toy with "estrogen receptors," they might carry risks similar to estrogen replacement or birth control pills. Do women really want to pop a pill that manages to induce PMS? Are big boobs such a prize we're willing to do to our bodies hormonally whatever it is that makes them swell and ache for a few days every month? Either way, as my father used to say, "It don't look good."

"It's what we don't know about these pills that scares many physicians," said the study's author, Thomas Lawrence, M.D., chairman of the national Plastic Surgery Educational Foundation's Device and Technique Assessment Committee. Never mind that these are the same doctors who routinely fill women's chest muscle with saline water balloons. But, according to the study, fenugreek contains elements that can interfere with medications for blood clots and diabetes.

As for Lois and Bustea, a monthlong regimen proved futile. But after forcing the nasty brew down her gullet day after day with no results, Lois was more determined than ever. Setting her dashed hopes aside, she ended up ordering a selection of breast-enhancement supplements from the same company. These, too, failed to produce results.

Janet Evans has been a lawyer with the Federal Trade Commission for seventeen years. Since the rise of the Internet she and her colleagues have been on boob-penis overdrive. "You develop some bizarre expertise," said Evans, who described her own breasts as "nugatory." "There are lots of breast products out there, but we expect good-quality testing. If these products do work like a hormone, and most are selling phytoestrogens [estrogens from plants], anytime you get genuine hormonal activity that's a red flag. You can't assume it's safe, even if it's a plant."

The breast enhancement people and the enlarge-your-penis people are often one and the same. The FTC will never be able to keep up with them. It's easier to regulate companies based in the United States, but more and more Internet sites originate overseas. And someone has to complain for the FTC to investigate. "Primarily, people complain to us when they got ripped off—their credit card was charged and they didn't get anything," Evans told me. But they are less likely to go on record as being conned because their penises didn't grow. As for Evans, she was more focused on products causing significant economic harm. "You learn how to look at studies. You see an advertisement that looks pretty hokey, it smells bad, and you'll say, Gee, I want to investigate and send a subpoena asking them to verify their claims." Thousands of breast enhancement creams, pills, and potions are sold over the Internet alone. The FTC has a consumer protection staff of five hundred, only forty of whom are attorneys. And the conventional wisdom that deceiving people is not in a company's long-term interest doesn't hold in the Internet age, Evans said.

Some purveyors have collided with the law, but there are just so many of them the odds are in their favor. They get lost in the Internet sauce, and even if they attract the FTC's attention it's easy enough to shut down and reenter the market under a different name. One company that ran into trouble with the FTC, for instance, was Vital Dynamics, Inc., based in California, which manufactured the "Isis System" of breast enhancement. (Never mind that anyone launching a business with the initials "VD" has a few bugs to work out.) The Isis System of pills and a cream cost around $600 for a six-month supply. Print, radio, TV, and Internet ads promised "Fuller, Firmer Breasts in as Little as a Few Weeks . . . Guaranteed." Testimonials had women gushing about an increase from an A-cup to a B-cup "without surgery."

Like most nonsurgical breast enhancement claims, this was a bunch of hooey. But Vital Dynamics reared its ugly head above the crowd when hundreds of consumers complained the pills made them sick to their stomachs, triggered allergic reactions, and gave them headaches. Despite the company's promise, consumers found it difficult or impossible to obtain refunds. At the end of 2002, Vital Dynamics entered a settlement with the FTC in which it agreed to stop making claims with no scientific basis, and pay the three individual complainants $16,700 each.

I used to love the television commercials of another ubiquitous breast enhancement product called Bloussant. A woman is explaining how her Bloussant-enhanced boobs have changed her life by giving her a new, often confounding visibility. "This man is looking at me and I'm asking myself, 'What's he thinking?'" her voice-over coos while we see the man checking her out. "He's asking me for my number . . . What's he thinking?" This goes on until you either hit the remote or smash the TV set. After a high-profile run-in with the FTC, Bloussant has been chastened somewhat. A family-owned company run by three brothers, which also makes a virility booster for men and a nighttime aid called D-Snore, Bloussant revised its website to include cautions that the pills have done the trick for more than a quarter of a million but "unfortunately, not everyone. Even the pharmaceutical wonder drugs don't work for everyone."

But Bloussant remains one of the most heavily marketed herbal breast enhancement products. It shows up in display ads in *Elle* and *Allure* and infomercials on thirty major cable stations. Not to be outdone by competitors, Bloussant promises an increase of two full cup sizes by "stimulating breast cells to regenerate the growth process." Put another way, to "regenerate the growth process" is to get fat. At the time Bloussant settled the FTC charges against it in 2003, sales of the product had exceeded $70 million.

I'd grown pretty much convinced that any woman who believes that she can significantly enhance her breasts without surgery deserves not just a slap on the back, but a slap upside the head. That was before I met Dr. Roger Khouri, the inventor of the Brava Breast Enhancement and Shaping System.

Brava is not only endorsed by plastic surgeons and other physicians but also marketed by them. It claims to be based on young but reproducible science in the field of tissue regeneration. Most important, Brava is the brainchild of a respected plastic surgeon who has had it up to here with boobs. Not only does he refer to boobs as "stupid mounds of flesh," Khouri has grown weary of bright, accomplished women submitting to anesthesia and surgery for the sole purpose of getting a D-cup. It ultimately struck him as pitiful, which is why these days his practice is devoted mainly to hand surgery.

Khouri developed the Brava Breast Enhancement and Shaping System for two reasons. Since big-boob lust shows no signs of abating, he wanted to offer women an alternative to surgery that actually yields results. And he wanted to make a pile of money. But I remained skeptical. Despite the sophisticated science behind it, Brava struck me as crude. It is essentially a bra with two vacuum cleaners for cups. And wouldn't women with the means to buy the Brava system be the same ones who can afford cosmetic surgery? Is Brava another fleeting detour on the road to surgery?

Before I visited Khouri at his home in Key Biscayne, Florida, I read many of the testimonials on the pink-infused Brava website. The system, which in use looks like a contraption out of *Our Man Flint,* includes a pair of domes, some tubing, and a data box with a phone hookup. It costs $1,200. That would be a lot of money for something that doesn't work. Consumers might be sheepish about the failed promises of a breast enhancing cream or supplement, but when someone shells out more than a thousand bucks they'd insist on results, or so you would think. Since it has received almost unanimously favorable press, either Brava really works, or otherwise smart women are far too ashamed to admit that they're a thousand dollars short and two cups flat.

Of course, there is another explanation for why no disappointed women have come forward. As its purveyors state emphatically, for the system to work a woman must use it, day after day, for ten-hour stretches, for several months. "It's like an exercise machine," Khouri says. "It doesn't work if it's under the bed."

Once I got a look at an actual Brava system, I realized that expecting people to use it as directed is like expecting them to spend ten hours a day walking around in nose plugs and flippers. But I'll get back to that.

Key Biscayne is a narrow island that sits in Biscayne Bay between downtown Miami and the colorful sprawl of Miami

Beach. It is not a community one would pass through. You reach it by going over a causeway. When you reach the end you must go back the way you came. The place reeks of wealth. Khouri's house is modern, boxy affair on the bay. At one point he excused himself to go to another part of the house to get me a copy of one of his papers, and I saw him walk to the hallway and press a button for an elevator. We sat with coffee in a kitchen with a view of the pool and the choppy open water just beyond it. The day was unseasonably cold for Miami, not more than 40 degrees, and like all Floridians, he seemed apologetic about this.

Khouri is a balding, fit man in his late forties and married to a dermatologist. As a hand surgeon, he no longer devotes his energy and skills to clients wanting to improve their looks. He performs delicate, demanding, and time-consuming surgery to put people back together after horrendous injuries. He now sits on Brava's executive board but plays no part in its day-to-day business.

"I trained at NYU with William Shaw, the guru of micro-surgery and a pioneer in reconstructive breast surgery," Khouri began. "This is surgery that removes tissue from one part of the body to another, where it renews circulation. The method took off in the eighties and was used mainly to cure wounds. It's not like a graft, which survives over healthy muscles. For tissue transfer you need meat, tissue with tiny blood vessels. When I left NYU for Harvard, I was doing mostly hand surgery, but my practice shifted to breast surgery. That's because I was the only one who knew this technique, who learned tissue trans-plantation from the guru, so I could go to the belly, the but-tocks, wherever there's tissue, and transplant it to the breasts."

This was at the time when silicone breast implants got a bad name. Khouri attributed the uproar over silicone to "mass hysteria," but women wanted the implants removed because of what they'd read about them. "So in women who'd had mastectomies [but desired an alternative to silicone implants] I'd do the reconstruction and some cosmetic work," he went on. "Most of the women were happy to get a tummy tuck as a bonus. In others, we took the tissue from the butt."

As Khouri's reputation as a breast man put him at the top of his profession, he was privately growing troubled about the demand for his skills, especially among women who were not cancer survivors. Women flocked to him and said, Make me beautiful. And Khouri had an epiphany. It struck him like a wallop from an encapsulated E-cup. "What really struck me when I was doing all that breast reconstruction was, number one, the importance of the breast in a woman's self-image. I wasn't seeing a cross-section of women but within that sample it was amazing that all these women were willing to go through this procedure to have those big mounds on their chests. Number two, it was too much surgery. I'd think about the fact that I've done all this, just to make a mound on the chest. So much suffering and risk. It just evaded me, how important it was."

Still, Khouri felt there should be an alternative. "It amazes me what women go through—the drugs, the pain." At the time he was doing so much breast surgery, Khouri was also overseeing a tissue-engineering laboratory in Washington. "We were working with growth factors, how to create tissue, like the kind in breasts." In his work reconstructing hands he was revascularizing—renewing blood flow to muscle, skin, and bone. Beyond that, he was versed in a technique that rejuvenates tissue by creating tension that stimulates that tissue to grow. "It's a gentle restrained tension," Khouri said. "The cells in our body are always under slight tension; this makes them thrive. It's like a rubber band that generates more rubber. In fact, that is how we restore the breast after mastectomy. We put in tissue expanders to stretch and generate skin. We create an inflated balloon and take it out surgically, then replace it with an implant."

The notion of creating breast tissue nagged at Khouri, who was sure it could be done. It was, as he said, a paradigm shift, a way of building up the breast without cutting the skin. Khouri was excited about the possibility but wary of what his colleagues would say. This was thinking way outside the box, or in this case, outside the boob. "Imagine," he told me, "a respected professor of surgery saying, 'We're going to suck on the breasts to make them grow.' It's not only a joke, but reminiscent of the old Sears, Roebuck breast pump. It's ridiculous."

On the other hand, as Khouri put it, "No one before had my expertise in tissue engineering. I have to have a streak of craziness to think outside the box, to really have what it takes—an engineering as well as a medical background." Khouri studied the physics of the problem: how much tension, where, and sustained for how long. "It's not a simple device to build," he said of Brava. "It took almost four years to build the first prototype. The mold technology was transferred from plastics engineers. The device has to interface with the body. When we use tissue expanders before surgery, they're on twenty-four/seven. So this thing had to work with sustained and prolonged gentle pressure, yet it had to be something women can wear for many hours a day, with no blisters or tears. I enlisted a medical student and an engineering student. The first prototype was rudimentary but it proved the fact—it showed that long term we could maintain breast enlargement. But I didn't think those results were strong enough to publish." Still, they were encouraging, and Khouri soon enlisted Dr. Thomas Baker, now in his eighties and an eminence of plastic surgery, to do the study, funded by venture capitalists. It was published in 2000 in the journal *Plastic and Reconstructive Surgery*. Among other things, this set the Brava system apart from and far above the slap-happy antics of Miss Khemmika, and the costly and lofty promises of Bust-Up and Bust Booster and Cleavage Extender and Rack-o-rama and Titty-Grow. Of the seventeen women in the modest study, five dropped out; the others wore the system from ten to twelve hours a day for ten weeks. Average breast growth was about 100 cc, roughly one cup size. A larger study of ninety-five women was equally promising. Brava also delivers what Khouri calls a "Cinderella effect," causing the breasts to swell temporarily and stay plumped long enough for, say, a cleavage-baring night on the town. Khouri's wife has used Brava that way, he told me.

I thought of Lois and Valerie. If they knew Brava would deliver results, would they be willing to climb into bed every night looking like R2-D2? Khouri didn't have a Brava system on hand, so when I returned home I called one of his associates and asked to borrow one.

The system arrived in a handsome black box the size of a milk crate. What would an utterly clueless person make of its contents? Some food processor attachments? A twin dog bowl holder? A heart monitor? An enema bag? Well, it wasn't exactly my problem. I carted the whole deal over to Lois's. I could barely wait to deliver the good news. No more vile Bustea! No more horse pills meant to convince Lois's menopausal body it was pregnant! Lois was excited, too. She extracted an instructional DVD from the black box and took note of how she would position the suction domes, secure them under the Brava bra, carefully affix the tubes and wires, and watch her boobs grow. She promised a progress report in a week.

When we met up a week later, Lois was not happy. Sleep-deprived and just generally fed up, she described a nightly scene in which the suction domes, perhaps homesick for their box, tried to bolt. Lois would wrestle with the Brava bra only to have it shoot across the room. When she finally got the whole business secured and managed to leave it on for a stretch, she ended up with a nasty contact rash. Unlike all the women heaving with praise in their online testimonials, Lois was not crying Brava. She was crying *basta*.

Might I make the brazen suggestion that life is too short for this? At least Miss Khemmika lets loose with one hearty whack and that's the end of it. But as for the search for bigger breasts on all fronts, so to speak, there will be no end to it. Hovering on the horizon, for example, is the possibility of using a woman's own stem cells to increase her breast size. I talked with a scientist who had already managed this in mice.

What's he thinking?

Downsized

ONE SUMMER WHEN my husband and I were renting a house in Woodstock, a couple we know came to visit for a few days. The wife, a highly accomplished scientist who was then in her sixties, had recently undergone breast reduction. Despite her eloquence on a broad variety of subjects, she wanted only to engage me in a discussion of her new, improved boobs.

"My breasts are self-supporting!" Rhonda gushed, thrusting the now demure C-cups in my face. She did look terrific, I had to give her that. Breast reduction is rejuvenating and it makes women look thinner. But, more significantly, it makes women feel thinner, and the thinner they feel, the better their self-image, the less they eat, and the thinner they actually are. It was also obvious that having smaller, perkier, and thus "younger" boobs had catapulted this woman's sex drive back to what it had been in her prime. I don't relish having to envision certain middle-aged people having sex, nor do I require them to consider me under similar circumstances. I felt myself to be teetering on a cliff, about to plunge headfirst into the valley of too much information.

Mostly, Rhonda wanted me to get my boobs done, too. She was very insistent, as if she were touting a new film or vacation spot. But the getaway over which she was waxing poetic involved general anesthesia, sutures, and weeks of painful recovery that might lead to . . . what? Prominent anchor scars and nipples akimbo?

"Trust me; you'll feel so much better about yourself if you do this," Rhonda had said. After bristling, as I always do, at any promise preceded by the words "Trust me," I wondered: do breast reduction patients receive a 5 percent kickback for every DDD they drag in?

In some ways I am a perfect candidate for breast reduction. My pair might be pleasing to others, but they also constitute a condition known as macromastia—breasts with weight and heft wildly out of proportion to one's frame. They swell, ache, and are painful to the touch for nearly a week before my period. I can never go braless, and in hot weather, the sweat on and around my breasts triggers itching, burning outbreaks of eczema and prickly heat. At times I've felt like forsaking the bra in favor of a wheelbarrow. I've had surgery for a herniated lumbar disc and my neurosurgeon warns me I'm one fall away from a double fusion on my cervical spine, severely compromised since a car accident in my twenties. The more pendulous my breasts, the more pressure on my back. I may be in for serious problems.

Breast reduction is an irreversible procedure that is more radical than breast augmentation, with a longer recovery period and, more often than not, significant scarring. I've never heard reduction mammoplasty referred to frivolously, the way implants often are. In fact, the procedure is often covered by health insurance if a large-breasted woman suffers from chronic back and shoulder pain. At 150,000 procedures and climbing every year, breast reduction ranks fifth among the most popular cosmetic surgeries in the United States. (It's only exceeded by liposuction, breast augmentation, eyelid surgery, and nose jobs.)

In a textbook detailing patient types for fellow plastic surgeons, my friend Bob Goldwyn writes that patients wanting breast reduction tend to avoid athletics or wearing a bathing suit. In addition to self-consciousness and shame, these women face physical consequences including back and neck pain, pain in the shoulder strap area, and obesity. Goldwyn explains that some huge-breasted patients consciously or subconsciously "gain great amounts of weight, perhaps in an effort to make their breasts seem smaller in comparison." For some young patients, obesity is "a way of repulsing men to avoid an intimacy that would result in exposure of [their] breasts," Goldwyn writes. Teenaged patients have visited him with stories of having their concerns shrugged off by doctors who advised them to get to like their big breasts because, later on, their assets would make them popular with men.

In visits to doctors over many decades, I never once thought to complain about the size of my breasts. Despite the unwanted attention they attract, I've always accepted them as part of the package, simply dressing to conceal them when I think it's necessary. If I lacked confidence or felt the need for an overhaul, whether internal or external, I never considered my breasts as part of the problem. In truth, I didn't give a thought to breast reduction until after I underwent back surgery in my early forties. Even then, it was the proselytizing of others that planted the thought. Having endured a few surgeries, I believe it would take a lot to shake my attitude that surgery is to be avoided whenever possible.

Besides, at fifty-one I'm content with my basic parts, flawed as they may be. Also, as I got older I stopped hiding under floppy tunics and box-shaped sweaters. I look my age and there's a sense of liberation that comes with that. I have a body. It is hourglass-shaped, sturdy, and compact. I am, as my grandmother would say, "shapely." Why continue to hide that shape, especially since I no longer feel so fragile?

Of course, some breast reduction patients make the decision before they gain the confidence of middle age, and without decades of toting DDDs around. Recently, I read about a thirteen-year-old girl undergoing breast reduction in Thailand. The article quoted her surgeon as saying that the operation was necessary even though the girl was still growing. It was as if this child's breasts were a menace that had to be stopped, and soon. Imagine being just thirteen and hauling a set of triple-Ds.

For some older women, too, heavy, pendulous breasts are nothing less than a pox on their existence. Lugging their outsized boobs around gnaws at their self-esteem the way their bra straps gnaw at their shoulders. If, like my friend Amy, they had gargantuan boobs before they gave birth, then, after nursing, their breasts become as unwieldy as twin balls and chains. "My breasts got bigger and bigger until they took over my whole body," writes Anne, sixty-three, in a plastic surgery chatroom. I know one woman, the sister of an old boyfriend, who dresses only in XXXL T-shirts, either black or a sad muddy gray, her breasts a vague but voluminous shelf lurking beneath. She has a lovely intelligent face but the region from her invisible waist to her neck has all the definition of a tarp thrown over a woodpile. The last time I saw her, it occurred to me that I may be big, but I'm not that big. I can stand up straight. I can wear tailored clothes. Though they make me feel like Little Annie Fannie, I wear bathing suits. Here is a woman who looks eternally uncomfortable. I have a hunch she would be transformed both inside and out by breast reduction.

Eavesdropping on some online breast reduction chat, I read posting after posting gleefully declaring newfound boob love. Drawn to the confessions of twenty-three-year-old Sarah, I contacted her and we arranged to speak. A lively, self-confident native of Newton, Massachusetts, Sarah works as a Web designer and lives with her boyfriend in Somerville, outside Boston. She has a ton of friends both in real life and online, and she'd probably wince at that distinction. "I am of the Internet generation," she told me. "I love the Internet, I have no problems saying anything online, and it was this combination of loving the Internet and loving people that made me tell my story on different chat rooms. I've e-mailed with women who are pre-op and women who are post-op, also known as OTR—over the rainbow—and I'll send pictures if it helps. Some women have infections, or had to go back for revisions, but you never hear any of them say it's not worth it."

Sarah e-mailed me before and after photos. She had been a 38G (DDDD), she told me, and her breasts hung so low that finding a bra, a bathing suit, or even a dress that fit was impossible. She learned to joke about her breasts and, rather than trying in vain to hide them, she made them part of her act. Sarah was smart and gifted enough to know early on that far fewer people would dare taunt her about her breasts if she made fun of them first.

When I saw her "before" picture, I gasped. It was painful just to look at; the breasts sagged with a weariness that made it seem they actually were heading to the floor, and soon. They didn't look like my breasts, though she was just one D beyond me. Because her skin lacked elasticity, a family trait shared by her mother and grandmother, her breasts looked, frankly, as if they belonged to an old lady.

After shopping around, Sarah chose a Boston surgeon

named Donald Morris, who had recently perfected a reduction procedure tailor-made for her. It was for women with pendulous breasts who desired breasts that were smaller and less unwieldy, but still big. Sarah is a D-cup now. "I wanted to still have big breasts," she said. "That's who I am." Dr. Morris sliced around Sarah's areolas and made two cuts, one below each breast, and one mid-breast where the bottom of each new breast would reside. After scooping out the tissue between the lines he made a hole above each new breast line, poked the loose nipple up and out through each breast, and sewed the nipples on in their new and higher perch. In the "after" pictures, Sarah's nipple scars have faded to the point where it looks as if someone traced the areolas with a pale red crayon. The scars beneath each breast aren't visible at all.

"They're perfect," Sarah said, six months after surgery. "I love them. I loved being naked before, but I really love being naked now. I can exercise and be healthy. I can run." On a recent shopping spree Sarah bought about twenty shirts. When a group of friends visited from out of town they had a party, and part of the entertainment came when Sarah took out her old bras for show-and-tell. For the rest of the evening her friends wore the bras on their heads.

My hiking partner Carolyn had her breasts reduced to a C-cup when she was seventeen. For the few years she bore them, her breasts caused her nothing but embarrassment and pain. Today, at twenty-four, she has one regret: that she didn't get more taken off. At sixteen, already a DDD on an otherwise tiny frame, she'd been molested by a boyfriend, and other boys at school displayed their pubescent sensitivity by making bets on who could cop a feel. If she had to endure this in the confines of her teenage sphere, what awaited her out there in the real world? But was her and her parents' decision for her to undergo radical surgery made only because boys are jerks?

It was mostly about clothes, she says now. "I wanted to go with my friends to Disney World and I couldn't find a bathing suit. My body was so out of proportion. It wasn't even about being overweight; it was about having such a small back and shoulder width with such a large load. I could do everything, but I was kicked off the volleyball team because my coach thought I was too large to play my position. I would look at clothes in stores and be like, God I wish I could wear this, I wish I could dress like other people."

Carolyn's father is a doctor. From the time her breasts began to wax beyond the age-appropriate, his concern had a clinical aspect. Her pediatrician concurred that there was a problem. And while it could do nothing to change a teenager's eye color or the length of her legs, modern medicine offered a solution to what, in the opinion of surrounding adults, was wrong about Carolyn.

"I was so embarrassed and ashamed that I was getting this done," she says. "I was like, How am I ever going to tell my boyfriends about this in the future, are they going to think less of me? You have to remember how young I was; the first visits to the doctor were so degrading. They had to measure me and take molds and were talking into a tape recorder for the insurance, and saying how my body was so out of proportion and ugly and wrong, and I'm seventeen! Hello! I'm still in the room! The doctor said he couldn't guarantee I could nurse my children, have sensation in my boobs. He said I couldn't go on the pill, that I'd have scars for the rest of my life. But he was also saying, I fully recommend this or else I'll be seeing you back here at thirty for back surgery."

Breast reduction surgery has been done in America for fifty years and the procedure has remained pretty much the same.

It's only recently that doctors are offering gentler alternatives with less scarring. More and more women are looking not just for reduction but also for a lift. They want boobs that are not just smaller but perkier. If they're my age or older, they envision themselves with the boobs of a twenty-year-old, gravity be damned.

One look at the telltale "anchor" scars—an upside-down T on the bottom half of each breast—and you can see clearly how the job is done. The surgeon cuts along the bottom of the areola and makes an incision vertically below it to the breast crease. After removing some breast tissue and skin he or she repositions the nipple to a higher site. In the process the surgeon can even out breasts that are noticeably asymmetrical. There are methods that leave less scarring, but these are new, and the surgeons performing them are likely to be new to the procedure as well.

The most recent development is the "Stevens Laser Bra," developed by Dr. Grant Stevens of Marina Plastic Surgery Associates. Known as the Laser-assisted Internal Fabrication Technique, or, no kidding, LIFTSM, the procedure is, like its predecessors, done under general anesthesia. As with Sarah's surgery, incisions conform to the contour of the breast. The breasts along with the nipples are lifted, and excess fat, tissue, and skin carved from the sides. Wielding a carbon dioxide laser, the surgeon further reduces and works the exposed breast tissue, and the laser softens the skin enveloping the breast. The "bra" is formed from the internal scarring that results from all this jabbing and prodding, so to call it a bra is rather like calling a hip replacement a girdle. According to Stevens, the laser bra prevents the occurrence of a common but pesky aftereffect known as fallout, in which the lower part of the reduced breast begins to drop.

No matter what the reduction procedure, the recovery period is, by all accounts, as long as a year and, for some women, pretty awful. "That first week home you look down and you're a bloody mess," Carolyn recalls. "It just looked like a nightmare." Goldwyn warns fellow surgeons about this period: "You had expected gratitude for relieving [the patient] of her deforming burdens. She is now perplexed and disappointed as you stand uneasily at the bedside. Before you become angry and stomp out of the room, remember that she had to make a major adjustment to her body image. Unlike the patient after a facelift who remembers when she was young, the big-breasted patient, especially if middle-aged or older, may never recall having a normal bosom. . . . If she had intended to lose weight, gently remind her that you have gauged her surgery to match what she will look like. . . .

"Your statement to her brings to mind the exchange between Pablo Picasso and Gertrude Stein, who said, after she saw his portrait of her, 'It doesn't look like me,' to which Picasso replied, 'It will.' "

Carolyn remembers graduating from sports bras to bras in her new diminished size. "When I put on my first C-cup bra I said, Wow, I can't believe I'm this small," Carolyn tells me. "But I have days when I wish they'd made me smaller. I get whistled at on the street—I'm still tiny waisted with big boobs—and I still wish I was made smaller to avoid that unwanted attention that big boobs get you. It doesn't matter how you dress, you're still going to get stares. I like to work out, but it's hard because even at the gym—they have mirrors in front of the treadmills—there would be guys there who just watched my boobs. My boobs have been pinched on the street. You just get tired of it."

Carolyn is almost obsessively self-conscious about the anchor scars. Any halfway attentive lover will see them and want to know what they're about, so talking about her breast reduction will always be a precursor to lovemaking. I tell her this is no big deal, but I'm older and wiser, or at least more fatalistic. I think of all the friends my age who gamely bear the scars of lumpectomies, or worse, and are happy to be alive.

Because breast reduction, though often covered by health insurance plans, is also a cosmetic procedure, surgeons are apologetic about the scars. Discussion of their appearance and how slowly they fade dominates the post-op chat rooms. But the newest minimal-scar breast reductions demand a higher level of surgical prowess. So it's innovators like Gerald Johnson, he of the "silly string" mega-boobs, who tout more aesthetically pleasing, if not widely accepted, alternatives.

"I hated that operation; it leaves the girl butchered," Johnson told me. "We don't do the scars. We have a new method; I call it suction without suction. You just go in like you're going to suction the breast [fat tissue] and instead of having the suction applied, you use the instrument itself and go back and forth, back and forth, and make rough areas so the breasts will grow back together in an elevated position." The method requires Johnson to go at the breast tissue at least a hundred times with a cannula, a narrow pipe normally used for suction and resembling a screwdriver. Johnson also does breast reductions by suctioning breast fat through a tube inserted in the belly button. While the breasts heal, explained Johnson, he "roughs up the surfaces" so the breast tissue will stick back together. If this sounds terrifying, that's exactly what it is to most women, who still opt for the traditional method. I've seen liposuction performed. It requires exertions that are energetic at least, and at worst resemble the bodily thrusts of an ax murderer. Most surgery carries unspoken overtones of violence and mutilation, which is one reason we are made to sleep through it. Liposuction in particular looks like something invented to force confessions out of prisoners. Combine that jabbing with the distance from the navel to the breast and, well, best not to contemplate it too closely. "Sometimes you don't get the best results but there usually aren't any complications with this," Johnson assured me. "When patients follow instructions real well, we know they're gonna turn out real good."

Johnson's postoperative instructions warn breast reduction patients that not following them to the letter is akin to tearing off a cast during the healing of a broken limb. The enemy here is gravity. Immediately after the procedure, Johnson puts the patients in a bra, which they must leave on for three weeks, even while showering, though they can switch to a dry bra as long as they don't lay down. After six weeks, the patient may lie on a bed without the bra for periods no longer than a half hour. The wounded breasts are said to heal at about four months.

The most radical cosmetic breast reduction I know of was performed on my friend Lisa. Lisa is in the midst of a series of sex-change surgeries and is now called Troy.

What is the proper and polite response to being told a friend is planning a sex change? Letitia Baldridge and Emily Post are silent on the subject. When my friend Lynn informed me, as we stood in the parking lot of the local Grand Union, that she had news—her partner, Lisa, was now a man—I was uncharacteristically speechless. All I could think to say was "Can I have her earrings?"

At the time Lisa and Lynn, a petite blue-eyed Welsh woman, had been a couple for years. They moved to town together to open a shop. Lisa always struck me as confident and content, definitely on the butch side but not masculine, and completely devoted to Lynn, who'd left her husband shortly after she and Lisa met. I had no idea that Lisa was going through this torment. Though she hid it well, Troy later told me that as a young girl she had vowed to herself that someday she would be a boy, no matter what it took.

"One of my very earliest memories is of trying to pee standing up. My mom caught me and beat the holy crap out of me." As a developing teenager, she ignored her C-cup breasts in the hope they'd go away. "When my mom made me wear dresses I felt like a man in drag," Troy told me. "I ignored my breasts to the point where I could no longer ignore them." Though Lisa never had sex with a man, she dated some especially timid ones, and concluded they were turned off by her aggressiveness, which was a reflection of the boy she felt herself to be.

As a young lesbian in Los Angeles, Lisa fell in with friends who accepted her no matter how butch she dressed and couldn't have cared less whether she wore a bra or not. But when she joined a gym she couldn't bring herself to change in the women's locker room. "I felt like an imposter," Troy told me. "I thought, if these women knew who I was they'd be mortified. I was a man in a female locker room and that was wrong."

A little over a year after I ran into Lynn in the supermarket parking lot, a year during which he'd undergone the required psychotherapy and hormone therapy, Troy had his "top surgery." He felt a sense of urgency about this: he had been injecting himself with enough testosterone to stop menstruating and grow facial hair, but those C-cup breasts leered up at him. The synecdoche for all things feminine, these breasts had to go; the sooner the better.

Troy's breasts were removed in outpatient surgery at a hospital in San Francisco. "I'd had this perception that my breasts were really huge, but they were actually relatively small," he said. "Because you're not trying to get rid of cancer, they can choose where to cut and how to reconstruct. If you're small enough, they'll do a keyhole reduction, go right around a nipple and suck the fat out. They have to move the nipple because men's nipples are quite a bit farther over. Women's nipples are at the tips of the breasts and men's are higher and more over to the side. The problem with the keyhole reduction is it makes the chest area sag, and you have to wait for the body to re-adjust and then remove and replace the nipples later."

Troy had a double mastectomy, during which the surgeon cut underneath his breasts and along the sides. "I had stitches from the cut," Troy told me, "but he did reconstructions underneath to make sure that the skin lies correctly and he was able to move the nipples and put them back on immediately." The surgery cost $10,000, which included a $2,000 fee for another surgery to correct "dog ears"—loose skin puckers under the arms.

I asked Troy whether he has any sensation in his removed and repositioned nipples. The doctor had also cut the areolas off so each of his new nipples was, as Troy put it, like an "ap-pliqué patch." "I can feel some touch on the nipple, but sensa-tion isn't something you're promised," he said. "I do find it extremely erotic when my nipples are played with and I have to say that even if I'm not feeling the sensation, the psychological thing of having someone playing with my nipple is much more powerful than when I had breasts. I didn't like my breasts, and in some ways I so much love my chest now that having my nip-ples played with is like having her [Lynn] say my chest is sexy."

Troy admitted to having felt really weird at first. "You're so bruised with all that yellow antibiotic stuff, and you feel muti-lated. The feeling was accentuated at that point because I couldn't see the man's chest. It was like a no-man's land," he said, without apparent irony. "I closed my eyes when Lynn changed the dress-ings. But as everything began to heal and I got the stitches out I was able to see, Oh yeah, it's really a chest. And when the nipple scabbing fell off I could see it was going to be okay."

It was a cold winter day when Troy and I spoke in his shop on my town's nearly deserted main street. Troy lifted his sweatshirt so I could see his chest, which now had patches of thin downy hair around the nipples. The chest looked nothing like a woman's. It is a man's chest now, but the scars are pronounced and impossible to miss. This is not the reason, though, that Troy didn't go shirtless on the town beach last summer. "I don't go shirtless around here in case I run into somebody I know. It's like I'm going to weird them out," he said. "But when we're alone over at Long Point, or on vacation, I go shirtless all the time now."

As I write this, Troy is in a hospital in Gent, Belgium, undergoing a series of complicated, risky procedures that will leave him with an appendage very similar to an actual penis. These expensive, radical surgeries fall in with Troy's lifelong plan to become a male, whatever the cost. But as far as he is concerned, Troy was already a man when he left for Belgium. Once his breasts were gone, there was nothing else he could be. Now, he says, he looks at breasts—his partner's, strangers', mine—as objects of affection and desire. As much as he despised his own, he loves to fondle those of his woman. At the same time the scars snaking across his firm pectorals tell the story of the healthy pair he was so impatient to shed.

As Troy bared his masculine, if not he-manly chest to me, I thought of Rhonda hanging around my kitchen showing off her new streamlined rack. If I had my breasts carved down to a demure B-cup, would I find myself transformed in surprising ways? Perhaps I'd mourn the loss of a key adjective in my enduring profile. And hearing these stories, I realized that as irksome as my breasts might sometimes be, I'd miss them.

What's Good for the Gander

I ONCE VISITED A public bath in Kuşadasi, Turkey.
Though situated in the shadow of a mosque, this *hamam*
happened to be a coed establishment. The "bath" portion of
the experience involved cowering nude in a steamy alcove until
a man in a loincloth slinked over to scour my body with a
generic form of Ajax. This was followed by a "massage" in
which another man yanked my ankles until my hips were
nearly torn from their sockets. He then pummeled my naked
flanks with a water-filled sack of some kind. I tried to escape
but yet another man, snarling "Not finish!" got me in an arm-
lock and announced it was time to "wash hair." Like a delous-
ing nurse at a reform school in hell, he attacked my head with
more of the caustic soap powder.

What lingers most clearly in my memory is what happened
afterward. Still nude, with our hair resembling Medusa's crown
of snakes and our skin rubbed red and raw, my companions and
I had to walk the length of an elegantly appointed atrium and
up a flight of stairs to changing rooms situated along a mezza-
nine. Around this atrium sat fully clothed Turkish men smoking

and drinking tea. Our ordeal wasn't over. Given only one small towel with which to indulge any surviving shred of modesty as we walked past them, we had to choose what body part to cover. Without hesitation I wrapped the towel around my breasts even though that meant exposing a significant portion of my ass. In retrospect, and after enduring my husband's jokes that under the English "Turkish Bath" sign was surely one in Turkish that read "See naked American women and whip them with water sacks," I registered the fact that of all my female parts, I believe my breasts to be the most provocative and the most obscene.

As a result, when women in the so-called topfree movement insist that "breasts are not sexual organs," I flinch. Of course, breasts play no part in the biological act of reproduction. They may help melt the ice, but their presence or absence has no bearing on the conjugal deed itself. Still, these women's hopeful commitment to gender equality for the shirtless seems to ignore or willfully deny the overwhelming force of reality. Will there come a time when American women may choose, as men often do in casual settings, to shed their tops on hot days? Can habitual, everyday exposure make breasts as sexually innocuous as elbows? May women look forward to a day when we are judged not by our boobs, but by the content of our character?

I doubt it.

But don't tell that to Sherry Glaser, Kayla Sosnow, or Elizabeth Book. These are just some of the people chest-deep in the crusade for topfreedom. Everything they say has the ring of logic and truth. But after their message is allowed to sink in, and I find myself musing about, say, sitting topless on a bench in a public park one infernal August day, I feel a rush of vulnerability and shame. This, despite the fact that in many places—New York State, for example—doing just that would not violate any existing law.

Boob-flashing strikes me as a problematic way of bringing men to their senses. The effect is usually the opposite. Still, in many cases, even if it's by simply wearing out the patience of the court, these topfreedom fighters are ticking off small victories.

Most want only to change public nudity law. Sherry Glaser wants to change the world. Planting her bare-breasted, 40DDD self in front of Macy's in San Francisco's Union Square in 2004, she called out to the crowds, "I need your support. Really!" A comedienne and playwright who lives in Mendocino, California, Glaser is the woman who brought us Breasts Not Bombs, a fledgling, informal, and slightly goofy band of protesters. They are not to be confused with Boobs Not Bombs, a fledgling, informal, and slightly goofy band of protesters. (When you think about it, the names of both groups pack about as much logic as, say, "Mallomars Not Anthrax.") Glaser's group is more active and better at grabbing headlines—in fact, Glaser is a headline unto herself. Half dressed and with her placard planted proudly in a giddy parody of *American Gothic*, she is a force, her boobs impossible to ignore as gravity has them grazing the elastic of her pants waist. In the wake of each demonstration, Internet chat rooms are abuzz with ridicule not of Glaser's message, but of her physique. The writers, mostly men, are even less charitable in commenting on Glaser's partner, Sheba, who is not just topless but tattooed, pierced . . . and bearded. The slurs would be more distressing were it not for Glaser's game, I-don't-care-what-you-say-about-me-just-spell-my-name-right attitude.

What reporter could resist this bunch, with their penchant for deflecting hecklers with calls for Titties Not Tanks, Nipples Not Napalm, Mammaries Not Missiles? (Glaser's other motto is "The issue is soft tissue.") Faced with arrest on the eve of a planned state capitol protest, Glaser pointed a finger right back and said, essentially, Excuse me, but I'd like to point out the real meaning of "obscene." "The women from Breasts Not Bombs are being threatened with arrest for obscene and offensive behavior when we are looking at government officials who lie to grand juries, leak top secret information that compromises the security of the United States, launder money, fix intelligence to justify invading a sovereign nation, maintain secret detention centers, exercise torture violating the Geneva Convention. We are asking the question, What is obscene? What is indecent? Why are our breasts so threatening?"

As my daily influx of Google "breast alert" e-mails attests, everyone loves a good boob story. Though Glaser never got an answer to her question, she did get mentions in news reports from Kyoto to Dubai. At the antiwar protest in front of Macy's Glaser was joined by her ten-year-old daughter Lucy and her friends, proudly displaying their bare-chested American Girl dolls.

Throughout history, women have bared their breasts as an act of defiance. But a woman's defiance may just amount to a man's distraction. It appears that no amount of breast-baring activism can dull boobs' power to stupefy; it also appears that no amount of it will bend men to your will. In the fall of 2005, a group of bare-breasted women and women in bras protested outside the offices of the Gauteng province department of health in Johannesburg, South Africa, singing, jumping, and raising placards. The women were angry because they had been promised but later denied paying jobs after volunteering for the department for three years. The demonstration was news around the world. The women's demands, meanwhile, were ignored.

"Show us your tits." It's the jubilant rallying cry of spring break crowds, Mardi Gras revelers, biker roundups, and the touring production of *Girls Gone Wild*. But most women who call themselves topfree activists are not beach babes. This is not the implant crowd. These are normal, squishy, cellulite-pocked women. Many topfree activists are also nudists, which explains a lot. In spite of the overwhelming weight of societal fixations and fervor, committed nudists challenge the sexualization of the unclothed body and take righteous aim at—I'm not making this up—the "textile community." Other topfreedom crusaders are New Age–steeped earth mothers who long to expose all that is nurturing and brimming with sustenance and life. This bunch is as sexually provocative as a bowl of muesli.

Determined as they are, for these women the news is not encouraging. In a half-blinding explosion of strobes and stage smoke, a technical mishap dislodges one celebrity breast and the nation's in a tizzy. Many Americans can't say who represents them in Washington or find Afghanistan on a map, but everyone remembers Janet Jackson's wayward boob. Which is why, in the endless din of catastrophic news, topfree activists still manage to attract attention. This continues to be the case although even the most organized topfree demonstration never succeeds in drawing more than a handful of participants. Though throngs of women gleefully bare their breasts at biker rallies and gay pride parades, we have yet to witness the million mammary march.

The largest boob-specific American demonstration so far took place in early June 2005, when around two hundred self-proclaimed "lactivists" nursed their babies on New York's West Sixty-seventh Street, outside the headquarters of ABC News. They were protesting Barbara Walters's comments on the show *The View*, where the news icon remarked that the sight of a woman breast-feeding next to her on a plane made her uncomfortable. Though their working breasts were clearly visible, this crowd was not technically topfree. The following summer in 2006, about twenty-five nursing mothers protested outside a Victoria's Secret store in Myrtle Beach where a woman had been denied permission to nurse her baby in the dressing room. As the result of the outcry, a bill protecting the right to public breastfeeding was introduced in South Carolina legislature.

In light of the fact that a large percentage of young American women are walking around in clothes skimpy enough to be construed as underwear, it is useful to consult the legal definition of "nude" breasts. In most states we're within the law if we don't reveal so much as a sliver of areola. Because, as we know, the areola is, for obscenity purposes, a mined perimeter guarding the real goods: the nipple. The following, from a Brevard County, Florida, ordinance, is typical of statutes defining breast nudity as baring "the portion of the human female breast directly or laterally below a point immediately above the top of the areola with less than a fully opaque covering. This definition shall include the entire lower portion of the human female breast, including the areola and nipple, but shall not include any portion of the cleavage of the human female breast exhibited by a dress, blouse, shirt, leotard, bathing suit or other clothing, provided the areola is not exposed."

But "nudity" isn't always so simple. One of my friends is a cancer survivor who has had a double mastectomy. On brutally hot summer days she strolls around shirtless. What kind of creep would challenge her right to do this? If exposed boobs are the problem, in this case the issue is moot. She has no boobs. She has no nipples. She has . . . nothing. Nothing to stop traffic, nothing to make the Verizon guy fall off his cherry-picker. Of course, Provincetown, Massachusetts, where we live, is a freewheeling place, reputed for its openness. It's the kind of town where one might encounter a man wearing chaps, a dog collar, nipple rings, and little else. But even in places where the letter of the law includes the above description of "nude" breasts, my friend is off the hook. If she should be wearing a top, then so should men.

At first I resisted the word "topfree." It hit the same nerve as, say, referring to a fat person as a "person of size," or referring to an amputee as someone with a limb deficit. But I've been lectured enough times that I decided to capitulate. "Topless" invokes exotic dancers and otherwise sexualized images of women. "It's extremely important to me that you use the word 'topfree' and not 'topless,'" the activist Kayla Sosnow told me. "'Topless' is the absence of something that's supposed to be there. 'Topfree' is being free of something you don't want. It's totally different. 'Topfree' is not about sexuality, it's about comfort." So "topfree" it is.

But as for Sosnow and her fellow foot soldiers' claim that the movement is about comfort, I am not so sure. For small-breasted women it might be, but in what way, I wonder, would the word "comfort" apply to someone as well-endowed as me? "Comfort" is not the word that comes to mind when I envision walking around with my milky-pale flesh exposed and my mega-boobs slapping me in the face. I don't remove my bra until bedtime, and even then I do so reluctantly. To what lengths will someone go to insist upon her constitutional right to be uncomfortable?

In my own backyard, the Cape Cod National Seashore rangers have gone after women sunbathing topless on some of its beaches, while turning a blind eye at a few beaches where everyone knows they tolerate complete nudity. It seems as if few things piss women off more than being told to put their bathing suit tops on while men of all shapes and sizes cavort bare-chested. At a bar association convention in Ventura County, California, in the wake of several arrests of women sunbathing topless, the veteran public defender Liana Johnsson sparked a campaign to strike down, on constitutional grounds, the state law making topless sunbathing illegal. To drive home her point to the state legislature she produced a video of obese shirtless men lounging on California beaches, inflicting their hairy man-boobs on those around them. And as for worries about women exposing their bare breasts to children, this, as Johnsson pointed out, is absurd. Kids and boobs are an item long before any potentially suggestive beach encounter. But a hefty set of man-boobs—now, those might give a child the willies.

In a twist that heartened the topfree movement, not long ago a Cincinnati man was arrested for exposing his breasts. In the spring of 2005, a twenty-three-year-old named Jerome Mason was charged with indecent exposure after going topless on a city street. At six feet tall, Mason weighs more than two hundred pounds and was described by police as having "a full set of breasts." (Not two, mind you, but "a full set.") Arguing on behalf of his client, who faced thirty days in jail, attorney Michael Welsh pointed out that not only is it not illegal for a man to expose his breasts, in Cincinnati it is "not even technically illegal" for a woman to expose hers. Walsh was referring to a 1990 municipal court ruling which held that breasts, male or female, are not "private parts" under Ohio decency law.

Developments like these inspire topfree activists to compare their fight to the civil rights movement. If the movement needs a Rosa Parks, one candidate would be Kayla Sosnow. Sosnow says she can "absolutely foresee a time when women can go topfree. In 1919 women weren't allowed to vote. In 1967 blacks were forced to sit at the back of the bus." Sosnow has a dream:

"It's only a matter of time," she predicts, "before women and men enjoy topfree equality."

Sosnow believes that our society is much more ready for that state than it is given credit for. She has been testing the waters for some time. Habitually topfree at her Gainesville, Florida, home, she has answered the door bare-breasted to greet the UPS man, meter readers, clergy members, and the dog groomer. And she doesn't even have a dog!

I'm kidding. But one thing I noticed is, Sherry Glaser notwithstanding, humor and irony do not run rampant among the topfree crowd. "They just conducted their business with me and that was that," Sosnow says. She insists that not one even registered surprise. We'll have to take her word for it.

Sosnow is one of a growing, emphatic sisterhood forcing reconsiderations of the laws in New York, Tennessee, Florida, California, and Indiana, and in Ontario, Canada. I spoke with several of these women. But I found myself particularly drawn to Sosnow. When I heard her story I not only felt her anger, I was pretty certain I'd react the same way she had. At thirty-nine, Sosnow is what drag queens would call a "big girl"—wide-bottomed and narrow on top. Her breasts are fairly small, with large nipples and age-appropriate sagging. They're not porn-worthy but they're not a set of wind socks, either. Sosnow's thick frizzy hair falls to her mid-back and her skin is an unblemished pale ivory. Like many of her compatriots on the topfree front lines, she is 99 parts earth mother to 1 part vixen. She is also intelligent and serious, and she toils in the distinctly unfrivolous profession of real estate sales.

In 1996, Sosnow was in northern Florida's Osceola National Forest enjoying the gentle company of the Rainbow Family, a national alliance of free spirits from all walks of life. It was a sultry 92 degrees out when she and a male friend, both shirtless, went to collect water for their campsite. At the time nearly a thousand of her Rainbow comrades were cavorting in various stages of undress, but at the water tower Sosnow and her friend were confronted—more like ambushed—by the police. "Put your shirt on," a policeman said to her. The matter might've ended there. But the reality could not have been more stark: male friend shirtless, okay; Sosnow shirtless, not okay. "I asked, Are there any local laws or ordinances requiring me to put my shirt on? Why not ask my male friend to cover up, too?" Reacting as if Sosnow's tits were Uzis, the cop radioed for reinforcements. Within minutes he was joined by six police cruisers and several park rangers. Six police cruisers! Sosnow soon found herself in jail, facing interrogation about her sexual orientation and whether she used drugs.

Sosnow's release on $500 bail was the beginning of a grueling saga that led to a jury trial. She was sentenced to thirty days in jail, to be suspended after completion of five months of probation and fifty hours of community service. Then things got stranger. Apparently her community service choice of working with children was a violation of her parole. Out of the legal muck emerged not a hapless camper with her shirt off, but a sexual predator. After weeks of legal wrangling, Sosnow served sixteen days in jail. There she was, in the company of mother rapers and father stabbers . . . for committing an offense even milder than Arlo Guthrie's hapless littering. Eventually Sosnow's conviction was overturned, but not before she'd penned her own ditty:

And in this fantasy, I invite him [the judge] for herb tea,
and far from the halls of justice, I ask what all the fuss is.
Well, thoughtfully he sat, then said, "Mine are flat, yours fat
. . . and I think it's really shitty, that you showed the world
your titties."

But then I explained to him our quest, to gain freedom of
   the breast:
"You see, Judge, they aren't dirty. You'll get used to that,
   they're purty.
And who was it to decide, that by law females must abide,
Our bodies in shame we must hide? That seems most
   undignified!"

Okay, so it's not "Alice's Restaurant."

There will be no enduring folk ballads about the "Moravia Four," either. A motley group of nudists, the four women were arrested outside the Modern Market grocery store in a small upstate New York town one infernal afternoon in August 2005. The youngest was forty, the oldest sixty-one. Accompanied by a few male friends, the women insist they weren't out to make a statement. They just wanted some ice cream. A day earlier, in the neighboring town of Groton, they'd ordered ice cream with their shirts off and no one said a word, at least not to them.

Would there come a day so hot that I'd go to the town shops shirtless, a day so oppressive I would find it impossible, for health reasons, to don even a scanty tank top? Of course not. But these are nudists we're talking about. Not all topfreedom advocates are nudists, but almost all nudists are topfreedom advocates. Nudists can be a strident force in their own right. To them, we poor clad slobs are the Muggles, missing out on all the magic. Still, most nudists have no reasonable expectation of being able to stroll around stark naked on Main Street. To these women, however, shedding their tops is a simple case of good for the gander, good for the goose.

"The district attorney was trying very hard to find some compelling interest of the State of New York that we interfered with," said Carol Clarke, fifty-four, of Branchport, one of the Moravia Four. Clarke was arrested along with her friend Barbara Crumb, sixty-one. The village police told them they were free to go, but then the Cayuga County sheriff herded them into the back of a hot squad car, where they sat and waited to learn whether or how they had broken the law. "They tried to charge us for interfering with the collection of sales tax," Crumb told me. This was obviously reaching. And yet the pair was taken to court, arraigned, and released on $250 bail each. The whole episode lasted six hours. Several months and hearings later, the matter was dismissed by the district attorney, who admitted the city had no case but warned the women not to do it again. They are now suing for reimbursement of legal expenses, plus $1,500 each for pain and suffering.

"To me it wasn't so much a cause as 'What's the big deal?' There's no difference between me being topfree and a guy being topfree," Crumb told me. "What I get a laugh about is when people say they don't want their sons to see me like that, and I'm thinking, He's seen airbrushed breasts in *Playboy* magazine. Let him see a real pair."

Clarke was less matter-of-fact about the incident. "I did feel sexualized," she said. "I felt like I should be ashamed. I was very upset. While we were standing on the sidewalk being detained, a woman over by the grocery store had this look of horror on her face. So I kind of glared back at her, meaning, What's your problem? What? The look on that woman's face— that was probably the worst reaction I ever had." Crumb's resolve was never shaken. "I'm like, Look, buddy, it's your problem, not mine. Next summer when it's warm I'm going to go topfree again, because it's too hot to wear a shirt."

Among the feistier activists is Julia Goforth, a Canadian artist's model who is among the most high-profile topfree activists, and who is intent on going topfree in all fifty states. And then there's the headline-hungry Elizabeth Book, a topfree heroine and an ongoing headache for the Daytona Beach, Florida, police. Both Book's and Goforth's legal battles have been supported in part by a Canadian-based organization known as the Topfree Equal Rights Association.

The founder and head of TERA is a man. Dr. Paul Rapoport is one of those people who claims expertise in a suspiciously broad range of topics. Slight, white-haired, with a bushy beard, he pops up incongruously and often in the TERA website's numerous photos, alongside bare-breasted or nude women, waxing eloquent on topfreedom in a variety of surroundings. He's been at this almost ten years. It was in early 1997 that he learned of a bare-breasted woman charged with trespassing for refusing to leave a public pool about twenty-five minutes from his Ontario home. "I had more time than my friends did, so I started this organization to try to help that woman. People tend to think that a man advocating that women go topfree is just an opportunist," Rapoport told me. "First, we don't advocate that women go topfree, merely that they not be penalized for it. And, in my case at least, because I have seen many thousands of naked women and men in my lifetime, I have no obsession on the subject."

I asked Rapoport why he thinks people feel compelled to report topfree women to the police. "The most rational reason I have found," he replied, "is because it incites sexual lust in viewers. The way I'm thinking today is that sexual expression is complicated, and to reduce it by taking the part from the whole is to misconstrue the semiotics of the situation. What is signified by a woman sitting in her backyard, or even walking down the street without a top, next to a man walking without a top? I'd maintain that it's very easy to show that sexual allure is not what is being signified or even suggested."

Well, Rapoport's take on the situation certainly isn't going to cause any heavy breathing. I almost nodded off halfway through his sermon on what is and what is not sexual. But, like Sosnow and the Moravia Four, he is in it, he says, for the greater good.

"If people were able to see more breasts there would not be so much sexual obsession," Rapoport said. "It would be understood that breasts have other functions, including just sitting there doing nothing. Second of all, it would be understood that there are many shapes, sizes, conditions of breasts, and the continued assault on women to have cosmetic surgery would stop. There are many girls growing up who have never seen another pair of breasts, and they have been taught through media pressure that their breasts are incorrect, that something went wrong. There's pressure to conform to a model that basically does not exist. . . . It is a real problem, and if people could go to topfree areas there would be a lot less problems."

In his vision of a perfect world, Rapoport makes a good point. I must also agree with him that public nudity can go far toward putting a lid on rampant lust. I'm reminded of this after I spend even an hour on a nude beach in Truro, Massachusetts, a mile from my home. I don't just feel a numbing of the sex drive. I'm not even sure I'll be able to keep my supper down. For every fit naked person capable of even marginally turning us on, there are an equal number of naked people who walk that beach wearing either water socks or fanny packs, the effect of which sight, if bottled, could be the antidote to Viagra.

Rapoport conceded that there is no clear line separating natural from exhibitionist, but like the Supreme Court on pornography, he knows it when he sees it. He cited a case TERA refused to go near. "A woman decided to take her top off, jiggle her breasts, press them against car windows and say, 'How about it.' She was arrested and convicted."

While Rapoport makes his case in the lofty syntax of the academy, topfree trailblazer Elizabeth Book is sassy and street smart. A single mother who refers to herself as "the Wild Rose," Book entered the fray in 1998, when a female cop threatened to "put her ass in jail" for breastfeeding in public. "I said, This is bull," Book told me. The fine was $120 and the cops urged her to pay it and forget it.

Since then the fine has climbed to $253 and Book, who is forty-four, has been arrested several times for actions including topfree marches, sit-ins, and demonstrations to coincide with Bike Week, a teeming, annual ten-day festival drawing hundreds of thousands of motorcycle enthusiasts. The exuberant biker crowds echo with calls for women to expose their breasts, and the women happily oblige them. At one protest she was forced to stand on a flatbed truck, covered on three sides "like a friggin peep show." As the Fox News cameras rolled, Book heard a policewoman vow to "nail that bitch's ass."

Are nudity ordinances unconstitutional? Book's attorney, Lawrence G. Walters, a First Amendment specialist based in Altamonte Springs, Florida, believes that to censor topfree protests is to violate free speech. "We have tremendous protection for expressive activity, [in which] things that would ordinarily be prohibited, like nudity, are used to get across a political message, to get people to stand up and take notice."

Much of Walters's practice is devoted to defending topless dancing establishments. Outside the courtroom, he grouses about a puritanical society—ours—that persists in paying homage to a false taboo. If Germany can have clothing-optional parks that don't produce corrupted children and sexual mayhem, not to mention that topless females are a common sight on beaches throughout Europe, what is our problem?

"We're a nation that came from religious zealots," Walters says. "The censors always use protecting the children as an excuse for restricting speech, but research shows it's bad to shield kids from the human body. This whole concept of preventing a child from seeing a woman's breast—the degradation of women may be caused largely from this false taboo. And it's tremendously insulting to males. We live in a society where sexuality and eroticism is rampant in the media and we don't have people watching these titillating shows going about and raping women; we've gotten beyond that. Men won't be resorting to criminal behavior."

Walters points out that nowhere in the Bible will you find that nudity is a sin. This is our societal norm; therefore it must be preserved, people say. But plenty of former norms have changed. It's time, he believes, for some of these taboos to be reevaluated. Women are treated differently from men when it comes to toplessness, but treated the same as men when it comes to keeping their pants on. "It takes somebody to start the change, to drink from the restricted water fountain," Walters says. "I'm on the front of the culture war."

And so the culture war rages on, one pair at a time. It is not my battle, but I wish these women luck. Female modesty is not a front on which reason prevails. I recall once at a dinner party mentioning the women of North Africa's Tuareg people, who must cover everything except one eye.

"Why?" someone at the table asked.

"Because they need to *see*," my husband replied.

Me, Uncovered

M Y ADVENTURE HAS brought me into close, at times intimate contact with all kinds of boobs. I have gazed upon and occasionally had the opportunity to run my fingers across breasts that were augmented, reduced, or otherwise transformed. Blindfold me and by touch alone I believe I can tell the difference between saline, silicone, and old-fashioned adipose. I've been afforded up close viewings of female breasts on men and male breasts on women. I've seen uniboobs, franken-boobs, boobs with ptosis, and boobs like hoses. I've considered boobs inflamed from the suction of an enhancement pump, raw from nursing, weary from age, boobs pierced through the nipples and linked by a chain.

As a teenager I became familiar with the pinched flesh where my grandmother's breast used to be, and I've since grown ac-quainted with anchor scars, lollipop scars, nipple sutures, and scars along the armpit. Friends of all ages and girths have been good-natured enough to bare their breasts to me, reinforcing my belief that when it comes to the real ones, no pair is exactly alike and each pair has its virtues.

In the process I've grown rather fond of my own boobs, my good old girls. As I massage them with coconut oil after my bath, I find myself less and less averse to my breasts' imposing fleshy contours and less concerned about their inexorable migration south. I've come to admire their softness and resilience even though they are destined to morph into limp appendages with the erotic allure of turnips. They continue to astound me. After being smashed impossibly flat between the mammographer's plates all those times, they still spring back to their pencil-grabbing glory. They remain useful, if only for entertainment value. I continue to crack my husband up by smushing them against the glass of the front door when he comes home with the groceries. When my granddaughter and I have belly-dancing parties, I attach baubles to my bra and send her into hysterics with my feeble attempts to gyrate the beads in unison. Long after their centerfold appeal sinks into oblivion, my boobs will be making my loved ones laugh.

Who has gazed upon my own loopy treasures in the flesh? Only the usual suspects: two husbands, some boyfriends, female relations, girlfriends, roommates, women at the gym. I've never been particularly modest about my body, but I'm no Sherry Glaser, either. And yet I am writing, for the edification of strangers, my boob story. If my tits become objects of public consideration, I have only myself to blame.

Was that what I was thinking on the April afternoon when I dialed the photographer Jordan Matter? I came across a link to his work on the Topfree Equal Rights Association website. In addition to his successful business doing natural-light portraits for actors, Matter has in the last few years pursued a project he calls "Uncovered: A Celebration of the Women of New York City." Though it wasn't his intent, the series has earned Matter the acclaim of the topfree rights crowd, and I can understand why.

I clicked on one after another of his images of bare-breasted women of all ages insinuating themselves casually into public places around the city.

By "public" I don't just mean the women are sprawled between the boulders in Central Park or strolling along a deserted stretch of riverfront. These women shed their tops in the St. Patrick's Day mayhem at Times Square or skate bare-breasted along the crowded west side esplanade. A woman pours water over her breasts on a summer afternoon at a tourist-clogged Rockefeller Center. Another, breasts in full view, walks her dog along a congested avenue in Queens, and Matter has a picture of a slender woman, shown from the back, in jeans, naked from the waist up, hailing a cab at the edge of Central Park. A topless woman stands beside a laughing cop in Bryant Park; another exposes her pert breasts while browsing the wares of a Chinatown street merchant. An elegant but half-dressed woman and a dapperly suited male companion window-shop at Coach on Madison Avenue. Another image shows a hefty woman with huge sagging breasts fording the rush-hour crush at Pennsylvania Station. And then there's the middle-aged businesswoman in a pearl necklace who grips an attaché case while marching purposefully—bare, pendulous boobs asway—among the morning commuters on the Brooklyn Bridge footpath.

I fell in love with these images. I found myself liking and admiring these women whom I'd never met. Far from being even remotely lewd, tacky, or exploitative, the pictures struck me as joyful, tender, and great fun. Spencer Tunick might have us pondering nudity taboos with his Woodstockian tapestries of tush-to-belly naked folk, but Matter's pictures have a different, gentler resonance. They're an updated, giddy take on the Maidenform dreamer. What's different is, the half-naked woman with the attaché case and pearls *is* an assistant district attorney, or might well be. And there isn't one subject in Matter's photographs who looks uncomfortable in her body, whatever its shape. Though only a few are models, all the women look lovely, from the wizened septuagenarian on a motorcycle to the balloon-shaped brunette, pregnant to bursting, ravishing an ice cream cone.

I gave Matter a call and found him upbeat and unpretentious. He's the rare type of heterosexual man who can talk boobs without a hint of macho posturing. "I began the project in response to the Janet Jackson wardrobe malfunction," Matter told me, referring to the Super Bowl halftime show that shook the world. That debacle struck him as a corruption of the human body. But more, he was provoked by the ridiculous tumult that could still result from the fleeting exposure of one breast. "Uncovered" is his effort to demystify bare breasts. And if the *Today* show and the *Daily News* have come running for the usual prurient reasons, Matter is happy for the exposure, so to speak.

Though the end result doesn't show it, except for the few who are professional models, the women are extremely nervous before the shoot. Who wouldn't be? But then, Matter said, something happens. "They feel ecstatic. Giddy. Liberated." He doesn't pressure the women and has always half expected at least one to get cold feet. But none so far has. It's an adventure, it's not against the law. What's the worst that can happen? Matter recalled the excitement of one subject, a woman who admitted she'd never been topless outside her home. "Most are in no rush to put their shirts back on," he said. And as a New York *Daily News* article about one of the shoots attests, spectators do not hoot, point, swarm, warn of coming hellfire, or otherwise carry on. For the most part the reaction is a mere shrug or mute disbelief. Or people simply turn away. Spoken remarks run the gamut from "Whatever" to "Hey, it's New York City." As for men specifically, after spending a significant percentage of their existence undressing female passersby with their eyes, they seem chastened by the real thing.

Having begun the project with lithe young friends as models, Matter was soon searching for a spectrum of subjects, especially older women, with bellies and love handles, who might feel hesitant about baring their less-than-perfect breasts. He sees the project as a love letter to these women, and to the city itself. It is not illegal to bare one's breasts in public in New York City. Matter confirmed this, and when he's on the "Uncovered" shoots he carries a copy of a July 1992 New York State Court of Appeals ruling, *People v. Ramona Santorelli,* in which the court—the state's highest—concluded that "the People have offered nothing to justify a law that discriminates against women by prohibiting them from removing their tops and exposing their bare chests as men are routinely permitted to do." A few curious police officers have asked to look at the ruling. In other instances, business owners have asked Matter to move away from their shops or cafés. But overtly hostile reactions have been rare.

When I told Matter I was writing about breasts and breast obsession, he got very excited. At first, this was less a deep simpatico connection than it was that acutely contemporary form of instant bonding: The book is publicity for the photos! The photos are publicity for the book! It was during this frenzy of mutual admiration that I blurted the following: "Perhaps I could pose for you."

Anyone could have seen this coming. And yet I managed to shock myself. Was I nuts? Talking to topfree trailblazers, I'd felt so certain I could not, under any imaginable circumstances, bare my breasts in public as feistier women have done. This photograph, should it be taken, would be on the Internet, for heaven's sake. We're not exactly talking bigjuicytits.com, but who's to say my set won't find its way there? I might as well change my name to Suzy Stacked and be done with it. My husband, a cartoonist, illustrator, and sculptor, has filled many sketchbooks with drawings of me asleep or bathing, which is as close to posing half-clothed or nude as I ever get. I've never hired a photographer, as a good friend did, to shoot me spread-eagled in naughty lingerie as a spousal birthday gift. I feel indecent if I leave the house without a bra, which I've rarely done. I'll wear one even if it's just to walk the dogs. And yet, as someone whose clothed boobs have left a trail of havoc behind them, I felt a kinship with Matter's women. It was as if they'd been given the chance to act on that feeling I always get when men can't take their eyes off my breasts. "What?" I want to say, cupping and jiggling my boobs for emphasis. "*What?*"

Now Matter was asking me to give some thought to where in New York City I might like to bare these breasts. And I didn't hang up.

I grew up in a suburb of New York and consider it one of the world's great cities. When I'm there, my favorite thing to do is walk for miles, looking at people and checking out the shops. One fall day I wound my way from Thirty-third and Fifth all the way downtown, over the Brooklyn Bridge to Atlantic Avenue, where I treated myself to a kebab platter at a Syrian café and then caught the subway back to Manhattan. Beginning with that walk as a reference point, I thought of places in the city to which I habitually gravitate. The Brooklyn Bridge, of course—but Matter had already done a shoot there. Along Atlantic Avenue's cluster of spice shops, kebab houses, and storefront mosques—oops, maybe not. Greenwich Village—a natural, and I might not be the only topless woman in view. But Matter's done that neighborhood to death.

Then Matter suggested a bakery. I loved the idea. After all, I once wrote a whole book about the meaning of bread in people's lives. We had an enthusiastic phone exchange about the idea, and went on to set a June date for the shoot. "I can see you eating a delicious-looking pastry, or standing among fresh loaves of bread," Matter said. "Or surrounded by pretty cakes and pies." When he made these suggestions, Matter hadn't yet seen me. He had taken the measure of my personality and was, I thought, right on the money. Of course, I said, Terrific, and agreed to come up with a few of my favorite downtown bakeries. Though rather heavy-handed on the symbolism, I couldn't shake the image of myself topless and holding a lemon meringue pie in each hand. At the time, my only condition was that the shoot take place downtown. The notion of shedding my top anywhere above Twenty-third Street, in a forest of skyscrapers, or of exposing myself to a parade of bankers and diamond merchants, seemed unthinkable.

There was just one problem with all this. I'd mentioned it to no one. I knew that before my bare-breasted photo appeared on Matter's website I really should inform my husband. If some guy in an Internet café in Abu Dhabi or Bonn can click on an image of my tits, I think my husband deserves first dibs at least. But I avoided bringing up the subject. The reason, I have to admit, was that I still couldn't believe I would actually do it. And if I were to go ahead with it, I still couldn't articulate why.

I asked my agent for her advice. She is the most reasonable person I know and I half expected her to say, It's crazy, don't do it, you'll regret it. But precisely because she is so reasonable, she said, Let me have a look at the pictures on Matter's website. What she saw impressed her. Only then did it occur to me that I should appeal not to my husband the spouse but to my husband the artist. And so, one evening at dinner, as the June date approached, I told him about Matter's work and how maybe, just maybe, I'd consider posing for him. Howie looked skeptical, but I led him to my computer and began clicking on the images. As soon as he saw the quality of the work, and that the women weren't wearing bunny ears or licking whipped cream off bananas, he said, "Go do it, and enjoy it."

For various reasons Matter vetoed my bakery choices, and together we came up with an alternative: Ferrara Bakery and Café in Little Italy. It seemed an inspired choice. I love this neighborhood and I've been stopping in at Ferrara's since I was a small kid on outings with my parents. My father grew up on the Lower East Side and imbued his children with great affection for the place. My high school dates and I used to go to Ferrara's for espresso and cannolis. Waxing poetic about Ferrara's, I thought of the pastries and sitting at an outdoor table on a balmy summer evening.

I did not think about sitting among the espresso-drinking, cigar-puffing men of Mulberry Street with my boobs hanging out.

The date we set for the shoot was one of the hottest June days on record. New York City temperatures hovered at 100 degrees during the day and were not much lower by night. The heat was so extreme as to be an event. It gripped the city in a way that brought many strangers together and turned others ornery and on edge. Matter and I arranged to meet at Ferrara's at eleven in the morning. He had asked me to bring or wear a loose blouse to cover up between sessions. I'd planned to wear jeans, but that was inconceivable in those temperatures. After much dressing and undressing, I settled on a pink and white polka-dot calf-length skirt, a cropped black cotton tank top, and jeweled Indian sandals. I brought along a roomy white cotton button-down blouse.

There was plenty of time so I walked to Little Italy from the West Village. When I met people's gazes I felt the way I used to in my single days after a sleepless night of bedroom acrobatics with someone new, as if I were harboring a naughty secret. You, sir, are off to work, and you, young lady, are on your way to yoga class; parents are dropping their kids off at day care and students are rushing to class. But I am on my way to be photographed bare-breasted on Mulberry Street. I am the only human in this diverse and noisy throng who can say this: I am mere moments away from stripping to the waist in front of people like you.

I arrived at Ferrara's early, took a table outside, and ordered a cappuccino. A few other tables were occupied by middle-aged local men drinking espresso and smoking cigarettes. In fact, the length of Mulberry Street appeared at that hour to be populated exclusively by men. Drivers were busy unloading trucks while proprietors of shops and cafés swept the sidewalks. Workmen hammered away at an open wound in the road. I looked this way and that, from one end of Mulberry to the other, and seemed to see only one form of life: male. The men at the other bakery tables looked up from their espressos to check me out. Like thousands of men before them, they let their eyes linger on my breasts. They were thinking, Nice tits. I was thinking, You have no idea. At the next table sat a well-endowed woman wearing a tube top over a bra with transparent straps. This struck me as an interesting and overly optimistic way for a large-breasted woman to resolve the summer fashion dilemma—a bra that tries desperately, and fails utterly, to be invisible.

This historically rich pocket of Lower Manhattan has become a metaphor for the world at large, in that Little Italy is slowly and surely being engulfed by Chinatown. Mulberry Street still pulsates with the national colors and garlic-infused smells of Italy. But a faint hint of sandalwood and ginger hovers at its shrinking boundaries. As the Little gets Littler, Ferrara's has become the neighborhood's heart and soul. I was glad we'd chosen it. Except that no way on earth would I shed my top in view of these men. We'd just have to wait until every last one went away, I decided.

In the flesh Jordan Matter looks younger than his website photo. A pale redhead with an impish smile, he reminds me of Sting. After a few minutes of chat Matter said, "Can you do me a favor? Go into the ladies' room and take off your bra. I ask all the women to do this, because I don't like the marks from bra straps showing up in the photographs." Uh-huh, I replied. Of course. In the ladies' room I peeled off the $150 red lacy push-up bra I'd decided to wear because . . . why, exactly? What difference did it make what bra I wore? I stuffed the bra and my tank top into my shoulder bag and put on the white blouse. When I arrived back at our table I already felt naked. In the sticky, unrelenting heat my breasts felt as if they might melt into my belly.

Matter and I drank our cappuccinos and talked some more. I learned that his wife was pregnant, and that she'd recently had spinal fusion surgery, which I'd been scheduled for myself but decided to postpone. At one point Matter cast a discerning glance around and said that we'd better get moving while the light was good.

"I'd like to have you eating a cannoli," said Matter. "Fine," I said, and he went inside and came out with a box of them. He glanced around again, toyed with his light meter, and said, to my great relief: "It's no good right here. We'll find somewhere else."

Feeling increasingly ridiculous, boobs flopping like flounders under my blouse, I walked alongside Matter as he studied the light, background, and shadow play at storefronts and stoops. He found a stoop he liked, within view of the Ferrara's sign and affording the deep neighborhood backdrop Matter prefers. He doesn't want the photos to look as if they might've been shot on a studio set. He wants a photo populated by buildings, traffic, passersby.

I wanted a Tums.

I leaned on a banister on the stoop in front of the Ferrara's sign and unbuttoned my blouse but held it tightly closed. Matter took out one of the cannolis, handed it to me, and instructed me to nibble on it and look like I'm enjoying it. Was it just me or was I, in a manner of speaking, licking whipped cream off a banana after all? We'd already begun to attract attention, which was not good. Matter didn't want a shot of me with a crowd of onlookers. He wanted everything to look as natural as possible. But people slowed down to stare. People were curious. They were curious because they saw a photographer trying to calm a woman whose blouse was unbuttoned but wrapped protectively around her breasts, and the woman was saying, "I can't! I can't!" Just then a moving van pulled up, casting us in near-darkness and disgorging two men and a couch, all headed for our stoop.

"C'mon," Matter said. "This won't work."

He put the cannoli back in the box and off we trooped. I felt sorry that I had dragged him out, but I didn't see how this was going to happen. Matter seemed unfazed and remained cheerful. Later I would learn that I had gone through all the predictable, normal phases of being photographed bare-breasted in public: Fear. Denial. Rage. Acceptance.

About half a block away Matter found another outdoor café with light and background that might suit us. We sat and ordered cappuccinos. The waitress said we couldn't eat the Ferrara's cannolis there, so Matter went in and bought another box. In terms of our mission, this café had something to recommend it. Though the table faced the busy street, it was also nestled against a side of the café that was a wall of brick at least five feet deep. This meant that I could shed my top while maintaining some illusion of privacy and safety. It was a subtle topless-feng-shui thing that made me think I might not disappoint Matter after all. Also, I was getting tired. I was feeling the numbing effects of the heat and the cannolis.

Mostly, I felt like lying down. Maybe this is how actresses feel about nude scenes after hours of makeup and blocking and stage direction: "Can we just get this damn thing over with?"

And so it came to pass that I yanked off that blouse and stood on Mulberry Street on a busy June morning eating a cannoli and licking my fingers while my boobs, which Matter himself was moved to describe as "really, really huge," announced themselves to the world, or at least this small corner of it. "That wasn't so bad," I said, buttoning up the blouse after the briefest exposure. "Oh, we're not *done*," said Matter. "I need to shoot much more, maybe try another location."

"Okay, *now*," Matter called. I tore the blouse off once more, chucked it across the table, and nibbled the melting cannoli. This time around I smiled. I'd blocked out everything that was going on around us. I was beginning to enjoy myself. Just then a well-dressed woman walked past us. And before I could blabber something apologetic she exclaimed, "You have beautiful breasts. Good for you!"

I took another break and then did it again. I did feel giddy and liberated and all that. But the feeling passed, and after a while I felt we were tempting fate. If we stopped right now, our adventure could be declared a success. If I kept whipping this blouse off, I reasoned, something awful was going to happen. I was reminded of the time I did the high ropes course as part of an Outward Bound trip. I'd been sent on the trip as a magazine assignment, so I wasn't intent on getting my money's worth in personal growth. I was strong and supple, and assumed I'd get through the course okay. But it's different when you're thirty feet up and walking what is essentially a tightrope. You're rigged into a harness and can't kill yourself, but the fear was like nothing I'd ever experienced. I quivered all over and my shirt was soaked through with musky sweat. I finished the first two sections and was nearly through the third when I fell. I managed to grope my way upright and asked the leader to lower me to the ground. *Now.* "Have you fulfilled your personal goals?" she asked. "You're kidding, right?" I said. "I amazed myself by making it up here at all."

That was how I felt about this photo shoot. I had underestimated how terrifying it would be. I did it even though I was terrified. There would be photos to prove it. Could I go home now?

Matter relented. "Okay," he said. "We can stop." He studied the images on his digital camera and showed me a few that pleased him. They weren't so bad. They were vertical shots that showed my skirt, people on the street, and a glimpse of Lower Manhattan skyline in the background. My boobs looked pretty solid, if wildly excessive. My face looked kind of cute. Most important, the pictures didn't make me look fat. I began feeling elated and a little goofy. I gave Matter a kiss and a big hug and skipped off toward my hotel. Back in my fancy bra and tank top, I felt both secure and positively irresistible. And though I normally despise photographs of myself, I was actually eager to see the finished image, which Matter promised to post on his website that night.

I couldn't wait. The next morning I signed up for an Internet station at the New York Public Library. Attempting a degree of stealthiness, I clicked my way to Matter's "Uncovered" page and searched the postage-stamp images for—Oh no! There was a picture of me, all right. But it was *just* my boobs and my head. No background. No skirt. The picture was, I concluded, grotesque. I was hideous, obscene. A gorgon!

What were my options? Though I'd signed a release form, I could plead with Matter to destroy the photo. I could change my name. I could move to Belize and be a jungle guide. Fortunately, before I did any of these things, it occurred to me to go back and click on the thumbnail. When I did, the screen filled up with the entire image. Back came the street, the buildings. Back came the polka-dot skirt. The picture was now populated by others, none of whom I noticed at the time. A couple a few tables away at the café. A workman. Drivers.

So the deed was done. I could add it to the list of things I'm glad to have done once so I never have to do them again. Rock climbing. That high ropes course. Riding an elephant. Seeing the Broadway revival of *State Fair*.

But would the experience resonate in any unexpected ways? Was it, as they say these days, life-changing? I'm not sure yet. One thing I did learn is, for all the lusting, leering, and hooting my breasts have attracted, my decision to expose them myself seemed to shift the power base. When I, of my own volition, remove my top and bra on a city street, if anyone is the aggressor it's me. How can I be the victim if I stage a preemptive strike? And Matter confirmed my suspicion that under these circumstances, the same men who stared hungrily at a woman's breasts just minutes earlier are suddenly frightened by them. Sherry Glaser understands this, I thought.

I wish I could report that the experience transformed me in an I-am-woman-hear-me-roar way. It did leave me feeling upbeat and somehow victorious, and the effect lingered for a day or two. (So did the cannolis.) But mostly it reinforced what I already know to be true: breasts are a big deal. An often inexplicably big deal. Whipping my blouse off on a truck-clogged street in Little Italy, I didn't feel defiant as much as adventurous, and naughty. But when I revisited Matter's website, the women in the photos, of whom I am now one, suddenly struck me as heroic. I know what they went through. I know they were squeamish, and terrified to do the precise opposite of what they always believed to be safe. I looked at their faces, then scrolled down to take another look at my own, and thought, Hooray for us.

Like a Natural Woman

W HEN THE CROSS-DRESSING Dustin Hoffman sheds his falsies and wig to come clean in the movie *Tootsie*, he confesses to a lovely, blameless Jessica Lange that he was "a better man as a woman." I love that film. It makes me happy and reaffirms my faith in purest true love. Then again, I am a complete goofball, who also never tires of watching *Pollyanna* and *It's a Wonderful Life*. In real life, if a man were to go about his daily existence, even for a short time, with breasts like mine, would he feel more empathy toward all women? Would he be more attuned to women's unseen but greatest gifts? Would he become, like Tootsie, a better person? Would he *get* it?

With the removal of his breasts, my friend Troy bade an irrevocable farewell to his identity as Lisa. When she awoke in Dr. Rey's recovery room with her new D-cup breasts, Roxana confessed to feeling like a "real woman" for the first time in her life. If breasts don't make the woman—as surely my friends who've had mastectomies can attest—it would be optimistic to deny that they still make a person feel more like one.

I have spent a lot of time in the company of male-to-female

cross-dressers, who visit my town in droves during a weeklong annual gathering known as Fantasia Fair, which celebrates male-to-female cross-dressers, male-to-female transsexuals, and the former on their way to becoming the latter. It's the breasts that confer on cross-dressers what they believe to be the essence and hallmark of femininity. Omit the boobs, and the entire effort, if you'll forgive me, falls flat. Being a biological female around these men has inspired a deeper consideration of what it means—and does not mean—to be a woman.

In time for the kickoff of the 2005 Fantasia Fair I printed a stack of leaflets headed "Let's talk about breasts" and deposited them by the welcome desk at Provincetown's Crown & Anchor hotel. Bonnie Miller Perry was the first to respond to my invitation. I called her as soon as I got her e-mail, and we arranged to meet. "I'm blonde," she said. "And I have breasts." "I'm short with brown hair," I said. "And I have breasts." To Bonnie, this fact alone constituted an instant bond between us.

Outsized or prim, boobs are an essential cross-dressing accessory. The makeup, the wig, and the shoes are all a crucial part of the package. Fantasia Fair has rolled around annually for the last thirty-one years, and with it come temporary storefronts hawking elaborately engineered lingerie. For cross-dressers, this is serious business. A true lady must carry her boobs gracefully, with a minimum of discomfort. She cannot be forever worrying that one or both will go AWOL. Nobody wants to go lurching after a silicone breast form as it bounces along a windy street. If at all possible, though the laws of physics are against it, the lady wants cleavage. For most of the cross-dressers, who include CEOs, commercial airline pilots, attorneys, state troopers, and a disproportionate number of engineers, cost is no object. What they want is the best pair of boobs that money—often a lot of it—can buy.

The event was already a tradition when I moved Province-town two decades ago, so I've had the opportunity to greet the ladies year after year, their arrival as reliable as the fall colors. Hovering close to Halloween, Fantasia Fair is sandwiched be-tween Women's Week and Entre Nous, a gathering of gay men bound, so to speak, by a common leather fetish. I have watched Fantasia Fair evolve from a glorified dress-up party to a multi-disciplinary event, with workshops, lectures, and seminars to complement the fashion show, FanFair Follies, and the awards dinner, where the ladies gush thanks for being selected Best Dressed, Most Improved, and Miss Congeniality.

As publicity about Fantasia Fair grows through the Internet, participants come from as far away as South America, Eastern Europe, and Japan. We see the fresh arrivals falling out of taxis under the burden of hatboxes, train cases, and outsized gar-ment bags. Increasingly the event has welcomed some drag queens, although Fantasia Fair remains predominantly hetero-sexual. Not only are most of these men straight, many, like Bonnie, bring their wives along.

Known affectionately among the locals as "the tall ships," the towering ladies are always a welcome sight, teetering along Commercial Street in their brittle wigs and ill-fitting heels. They are a warm, surprisingly open bunch. Though I don't feel com-fortable enough to tap anyone on the shoulder and say, for exam-ple, "Sweetheart, the baubles and earrings aren't working—pick just one," I have come to know and love the repeat visitors. For many years I stayed in touch with a cross-dressing surgeon my age from Washington, D.C., who took me to lunch when I was there on a magazine assignment.

Fantasia Fair literature describes Provincetown as a place with "no social limitations." Though an exaggeration, this is why most of the ladies arrive with their guards already down.

This may be the only place they can breathe freely while "dressed" in public. For this reason it is a thrill for the ladies of Fantasia Fair, who refer to each other by female first names only, to do the simplest things unharassed. It is bliss for a cross-dresser to casually and safely shop for shoes, sit at a café, stroll barefoot on the town beach, or attend Sunday morning services.

Bras, corsets, and how best to fill them are endlessly compelling subjects among the ladies. I remember one cross-dresser several years ago becoming transfixed at the sight of my breasts, to the point where it seemed as if some divine force were guiding him. I said, "Can I help you?" She longed to hear everything about them. How big, which bra, what style, what about camisoles, sleepwear? She wanted a primer on push-ups, and not of the "Gimme twenty!" variety. She was doing nothing less than picking my brain, as if I could impart the wisdom necessary for her to acquire boobs in the image of mine and care for them as I do.

The twin party hats this cross-dresser was sporting, perilously pointy and forming a shelf that looked as if it were constructed of Kevlar, were just wrong, wrong, wrong. There was nothing soft, feminine, or coy about them. He must have liked them that way, though, because fake-boob technology has taken us far beyond the quaint foam-rubber cones known as falsies. Would he be more impressed with my boobs if they were pointy, too?

The FanFair Follies and the fashion show draw large and benevolent local audiences. One year a wealthy Mexican cross-dresser in Oscar de la Renta couture had a mariachi band flown in from Tijuana to accompany her turn on the runway. Feeling like an android in my signature jeans, boots, and sweater, I've studied the parade of mostly dated, matronly outfits, poignantly

overpainted lips, and twin Mount McKinley prosthetic boobs. I
know it's difficult to find stylish dresses cut to linebacker proportions, but a spectator can't avoid help but suspect that most
of these men, when dressed, look like their mothers.

For as many years as I can remember, Fantasia Fair has been
headquartered at a sprawling inn and entertainment complex
in the center of town called the Crown & Anchor, alternatively
the Crotch & Ankle. Participants converge on the Crown from
many bed-and-breakfasts and small inns unfolding along the
narrow lanes that connect our old fishing village's two parallel
main streets, one of which hugs the harbor for miles and lends
Provincetown its legendary seaside beauty. Populating a barrier
spit at the very tip of the flexed arm of Cape Cod, Province-
town has long embraced individualists and people on the
fringe, whether artists, writers, poets, gays, or any combination
thereof.

Bonnie Miller Perry and I arranged to meet at her guest-
house, on Bradford Street near the center of town. I was expecting Bonnie, but not her wife, Sally, when I arrived in the
sunny courtyard of the Fairbanks Inn. Several notches beyond
being a mere cross-dresser, Bonnie, who is otherwise male,
does, in fact, have boobs. They are an attractive set of self-
supporting silicone orbs that thrust from the plunging neckline
of a loosely tied pink peasant blouse that brings to mind the
word "wench." X-ray thin, blonde, and heavily but not pro-
hibitively made up, Bonnie has paired the little blouse with
tight pinstripe jeans. A handsome but weary-looking Indonesian woman with copper-colored hair, Sally is buxom and
dressed in a tailored pantsuit.

There was a time when Sally naively assumed she knew
everything knowable about her husband, Brian. Today, fifteen
years into her marriage, it would be obvious to anyone that

Sally is not a happy woman. Her troubles began one otherwise unremarkable evening in 1998 when Brian, a wealthy, cultured bank executive, emerged from their bedroom as Bonnie. It had become increasingly difficult, and finally impossible, for him to hide the urges that had privately consumed him his entire adult life. Sally, who insists she hadn't a clue, felt deeply hurt and betrayed. It was at least as bad as discovering he was having an affair. It was like learning that her husband was in love with another woman—and *he* was that woman.

"I married a *man*!" Sally tells me through clenched teeth. Here is Brian, a once-divorced father of three, a worldly New Zealander who rescued her from a life of borderline poverty as a Jakarta hairdresser, adopted her fatherless child, and bankrolled a better life for her parents. Here is Brian, who brought her to the United States when his most recent employer posted him to Washington. And here is Brian, sitting opposite me today, looking a lot like Joan Rivers.

Bonnie has a lot to confess. Fantasia Fair puts the ladies in confession mode; it's not all frivolous girl-bonding and dress-up. Transgender researchers and psychologists with this increasingly common specialty converge for an agenda of workshops, lectures, and panel discussions. Workshops with titles such as "Whose Gender Is It Anyway?" "Learning to Be Human," and "What? Me Queer?" are for fair participants only. A few years ago I received special permission to attend a workshop on how to communicate like a woman. "You can join us," the instructor said, "but you must participate."

As the only other biological woman in the room besides Moira, the Midwestern linguistics professor in charge, I listened as corporate executives, physicians, and airline pilots in wigs, makeup, and skirts complained about the way their wives waste time and try their patience by not saying what they mean.

"We feel manipulated," remarked a six-foot-two stubble-faced insurance executive in a Peter Pan blouse. This is women's style of communicating, the professor explained. Women are conciliatory and eager to avoid confrontation. A man says, "What did you do with my glasses?" A woman says, "Have you seen my glasses?" Later on, the ladies were asked to role-play—first, a male boss firing an employee, and then a woman boss doing the same thing. Here they were as men: "You're doing a lousy job; you're fired, you're outta here." And here, as women: "You're doing a lousy job, dear. You're fired, sweetheart." The professor sighed in utter exasperation and turned to me. "What," she asked me, "is the very first thing any woman would say?" "I'm sorry!" I called out. "Yes, yes, of course!" "I'm sorry, I'm sorry, I'm sorry!" I left thinking, These guys may spend a fortune on clothes, wigs, makeup, and even surgery. But they will never get it.

Sally, the wife of Brian, er, Bonnie, wants back the man who was her husband. Now that her husband has breasts, that is unlikely. Apparently, Sally never heard the old joke "What's the difference between a cross-dresser and a transsexual?" "Two years." Though handsome and shapely at fifty-two, she looks as if she rarely gets through a day without crying. In the seven years since Bonnie made her operatic debut, Sally has come close to the breaking point many times. But in the fall of 2004, her husband did something that enraged and horrified her so much, she says, that she nearly lost her mind. He got breast implants.

I am sitting boob-to-boob with these implants, trying to imagine myself, a heterosexual woman, expected to live in spousal intimacy with a pair not my own. At least, compared to some of the work I've seen, Bonnie's implants look quite nice.

"Sally hates them," Bonnie tells me. Her tone is conspiratorial: we're all girls here. It's no problem addressing Bonnie, but

I venture into pronoun hell every time I ask Sally a question. Should I call her husband "he" or "she?" Or if I call him/her by name, is it Bonnie or Brian? Another cross-dresser once counseled me that the rule of thumb in the gender community is "Use the pronoun of the person you're looking at." So Bonnie is, unequivocally, a "she." But Sally insists on referring to Bonnie—to Brian—as "he." It's as if there are not three, but four of us at this garden table. It's giving me a slight headache. Sally's brow appears tightly knit by something stronger, perhaps a migraine.

"I left New Zealand in 1969 to work for a large international bank, first in London," Bonnie says. "I was based in Jakarta, heading towards a divorce, when I went for a haircut and Sally was the hairdresser. When I was young"—Bonnie is now sixty—"I married for social expectation and to have children—I have three, ages thirty, twenty-nine, and seventeen, who all live in New Zealand. But Sally was my love match." I hear myself make a noise to the effect of, "Aw, that's sweet," until Sally interjects wearily, "You always tell the story like that, like I ruined your marriage." She folds her arms over her chest and glares at the man who once swept her off her feet. "Why you do that. You say you had that marriage and then you met me, like that marriage wasn't over. I don't ruin marriage. It was over."

All righty.

Most of the cross-dressers I've met began dressing secretly as teenagers or even younger. But Brian, who had experienced a longing to be female decades before he gave himself over to it, tells me he didn't dare even to don a little mascara. In Indonesia he had the means to indulge, but he wouldn't allow himself to do it. "I was a vice president of the bank," Bonnie says. "I could not have done it." But living in the Mandarin

Oriental hotel in Jakarta; he grew transfixed at the nightly parade of the "butterflies," the graceful, ripe-breasted Indonesian prostitutes, who were whisked away in passing Mercedes
and BMWs. On trips to Thailand, Brian warmed to that culture's transgender "lady boys." He envied them as he did the
Indonesian prostitutes.

Bonnie would like me to see cross-dressing as a manifesta-
tion of enlightenment. Think of the Hindu demigods: male and
female reflected in one being. I'd heard this before, put in a less
lofty way—that cross-dressers, in giving voice to their long
suppressed feminine sides, are more evolved than the rest of us,
and twice blessed. But what exactly constitutes this "feminine"
side? Is it, for example, the impulse to nurture and soothe? Or
is it something a man of means can buy in the form of surgery,
lingerie, Pan-Cake makeup . . . and boobs?

Bonnie continues with her tale. "I didn't start dressing until
1998, but I first became aware of TVs when I was in London."
One day a delivery truck for a clothier called Evans Outsize left
a neighbor's package with him. Brian accepted the package and
later his neighbor's wife, who was suspiciously *not* outsized,
came to collect it. But instead of rushing off she sat herself
down and confided to Brian that her husband became a woman
in the evenings. Brian reacted to the revelation by feeling jealous and cheated. Why was he forced to "play boy" all the time?

For whatever reason, Sally never saw the change coming. "I
didn't get any sign at all," she says. "He was a man. I married
a man." "Oh, yes, I played CEO—the big man—quite well,"
Bonnie remarks. I ask whether she has a photo of herself as a
man. She doesn't, not at the moment. But Sally says he was very
handsome. "He went and changed his face," she says wistfully.
"He doesn't look good. He doesn't look healthy. Does he look
healthy to you?"

When Brian first appeared as Bonnie, Sally says, "I was three days crying." She had no idea that Brian had already ventured to meetings of the Washington, D.C., chapter of the Transgender Education Association of Greater Washington, where his yearnings were validated and his confidence got a boost. "I was surprised when I saw a book about male-to-female makeup. I was shocked," Sally says. He says they discussed it. She says she never had a choice. "He never tried to be harmonious with me. All he says is people have to understand *him*. Always *him*." At this, Bonnie titters dryly and leans toward me to whisper, "We like to say that we're not the ones in transition. Because really it's them—the wives—who need to change."

I'd heard this before. Some years ago I attended a Fantasia Fair workshop dealing with how to break the news to your wife. One after another cross-dressers and pre-operative transsexuals commiserated about their wives' resentment, and worse than that, their jealousy. Our wives don't like it when we look better than they, the chorus of cross-dressers agreed. "We went to Jenny Craig together and I lost more weight than her, which made her really angry," remarked one husband, clad in a magenta silk blouse, dirndl skirt, and gold-tone knot earrings. I was the lone biological woman in that room, and I recall thinking the men had it all wrong. Their wives are not jealous. They are profoundly weary of this new complication, one which makes the usual suspects—infidelity, unemployment, and chronic illness—pale in comparison. These wives may be thinking, If a guy wants to dress up as the woman of the house, let *him* change a diaper or mop the damn kitchen floor. If she spent that much time preening in a mirror, she'd be an object of ridicule if not disgust; when her husband does it, she is urged to assert her love and devotion by entering into the fantasy. This would be the same wife who, while she loves a good fantasy as much as the next girl, has to attend to dinner and to the kid who's down with the flu.

"My best guess," writes Helen Boyd in her book *My Husband Betty*, is "that cross dressing is a reflection of men's needs to experience the whole of themselves, and especially that side of themselves that is denied in a male-dominated society." But she observes that "the complications arise because men understand their own 'femininity' as men, and they know women through their own men's eyes. That may be why some cross dressers portray such a sexualized image of women when they dress as them. It may be why their notions of femininity seem a little absurd and outdated. Men objectify women . . . what else can we expect?"

What makes a woman a woman? In college I sat in on a medical genetics seminar that had us gazing at slide after slide of sexually ambiguous children and adults. Breasts and a penis. Flat hairy chest and a vagina. Strange genitalia in some limbo between masculine and feminine. Knowing such ambiguity, though unusual, can exist, I'm grateful to be a woman, unequivocally, through and through. I don't have to explain myself. I can lift up my shirt.

Bonnie/Brian can lift up her/his shirt, too. But it's not our cute outfits or lip liner or breasts that make us this way. Rather than being insulted by his/her pat declarations about the nature of femininity, though, I feel a stab of pity. A cross-dresser once said to me, "I'm just amazed at how comfortable you are as a woman." And I remember thinking, How comfortable, yes, and how fortunate. When we are at home in our given genders, it rarely occurs to us how painful it must be to feel you've been handed the wrong body. Compared with this feeling, some women's unhappiness with the size of their boobs seems almost laughable.

As Bonnie leans toward me to confer confidences, this funny feeling comes over me. I experience overwhelming relief, bordering on giddiness. As a woman, I can wear combat boots or join a logging crew and be just as female. I have nothing to prove. I can hide these breasts under a potato sack or I can milk them, so to speak, for all they're worth: this would be true even if my breasts were tiny. But to Bonnie, not announcing that perfect set of coconut halves, those boobs that came at such a huge price, is painful. I can tell she is perpetually aware of them. Far more than the makeup and coiffed hair, these breasts are her ticket to intimate sanctums like the ladies' room. One might assume that cross-dressers are fans of he/she/whatever restrooms. But for someone like Bonnie, a coed toilet would be a real loss. For the ladies' room is where women bond with each other over the sinks and fix themselves in front of the all-important mirror. I've emerged from public restrooms exchanging e-mail addresses with strangers, or exchanging farewell hugs. This stuns and mystifies my husband, who listens to me recount a woman's saga of childbirth or cancer and says, "How on earth did you learn all that in the time you were in the restroom?"

Bonnie has a lot of money. One thing she chose to do with that money was treat herself, her wife, and her sister-in-law to a cosmetic surgery junket in Thailand. They flew from the United States to Bangkok, where they met up with Sally's sister, who lives in Finland. Each had his or her own agenda, and the group list included facelifts, brow lifts, liposuction, and tummy tucks. They were up late the night before they were to check-in at the kind of lavish clinic that caters to Western "surgery tourists." The trio arrived at the clinic exhausted, Bonnie assures me, as if this were an excuse.

"Big breasts were not on my shopping list," Bonnie explains.

Whether Brian had Sally's reluctant consent is a matter of dispute. "I said *no*," she spits. But when the doctor said, just before putting Brian under anesthesia, that along with the brow, eye, and facelift he would throw in a boob job for $1,800, Brian agreed. It was a great deal considering this was a high-end clinic with thirty-five rooms, around-the-clock nursing care, and a clientele that was 80 percent American, many having gender reassignment surgery. "When I undid the bandages and Sally saw me for the first time—" "I almost died," she says, completing his sentence. So violent was Sally's reaction that her body refused to heal from its tummy tuck. Her wounds grew infected. They weren't draining properly. She was depressed and feverish, and her stay at the in-and-out clinic was extended.

"Can I see them?" I ask. And before you can say "capsular contracture," the pink peasant blouse has been unstrung and allowed to fall to Bonnie's tiny waist. She wears no bra. She doesn't need one. "Can I feel?" I ask. Evenly molded, impeccably round, with well placed nipples, the implants are as hard as baseballs.

Sally gets up to leave for a meeting. With pursed lips she offers her hand and says good-bye. Sally hates the breasts, Bonnie says, with Sally just out of earshot. "Of course, Sally has implants, too, so it's partly a competitive thing. I love to wear tight little Abercrombie T-shirts. And now I'd like them a bit bigger." The boobs, not the T-shirts.

With Sally gone, Bonnie grows wistful. Even as they struggle with her transition so far, she has secretly resigned herself to having what's quaintly referred to as the bottom surgery. She thought the breasts would be enough, but they've turned out to be just the beginning, the top of the slippery slope. "I never thought I wanted a vagina," she says. "I never wanted a man to stick his penis inside me. I always thought that would be disgusting. But I want to be treated more like a woman."

As I get up to leave, Bonnie and I exchange cards. Hers has a photo, smaller than a postage stamp. But it clearly shows her cleavage. How long can this person actually be someone's husband? Once in my car I absentmindedly cup my breasts. For the zillionth time I marvel at how these sacks of flesh can be the objects of such deep, persistent longing.

A week after our interview I received an e-mail from Bonnie saying how much she enjoyed meeting someone who, as she put it, "shares my obsession." She went on to thank me especially for touching them . . . her "two rocks, of which I'm so proud."

Near the end of Fantasia Fair week I received an e-mail from a cross-dresser named Dawn Marie, who declared herself madly in love with her breasts and eager to discuss them. She boasted of having the most beautiful breasts money could buy. These breasts, Dawn Marie said, make her feel content, secure, and deeply feminine.

These breasts are not attached. They are a costly and emotionally laden accessory.

Dawn Marie greets me in a crimson acetate shift, a soft black blazer, and the kind of low, matronly pumps that people of a certain vintage refer to as "sensible." Slim and shapeless except for a perky but soft-looking set of boobs, she wears a dark brown helmet of a wig coiffed to reveal pierced teardrop earrings. She's staying at the Crowne Pointe, one of Province-town's highest-priced inns, and clearly enjoys showing off the place. "And you should see my room!" Maybe I should, but I choose not to. Instead we settle ourselves on an easy chair and couch in the inn's plush finished basement.

I've arrived straight from a two-hour hike with my dogs, and though it's my habitual mode of dress I find myself apologizing to Dawn Marie for my casual appearance. I'm in jeans, hiking boots, and a long-sleeved T-shirt. "Well please excuse my outfit, too," she says. "I just threw something on." From a gay man, this would be a tart joke. But I believe Dawn Marie is serious. As we sit I notice that my legs are apart while hers are daintily crossed.

I ask a question or two and out pours Dawn Marie's story. Almost sixty and drawing a full salary, though she's been off the job since undergoing a quintuple bypass a decade ago, Dawn Marie lives near Fort Bragg, North Carolina, with her girlfriend of ten years. She refers to her girlfriend as her fiancée even though the two have no plans for marriage, which would obliterate the girlfriend's sizable widow's pension. As for Dawn Marie, she has a grown daughter from the first of two failed marriages, both of which succumbed to strain from her cross-dressing, or, as she calls it, her "gender situation."

"I've been dressing for as long as I can remember," says Dawn Marie. He was adopted in infancy; as a young man, he spent years in the Marine Corps, including a yearlong tour in Vietnam. While in the military, Dawn Marie dressed female only when off-duty, and very discreetly—for bed, in a night-gown and bra. "In the military, you can't stash a full wardrobe. You have to be very clandestine, very private."

But the bra was the key to her transformation. Early on she'd stuff it with tissues but eventually came to use "nylons," as she calls them. "They were my favorite." After the tour of duty in Vietnam, Dawn Marie quickly married. He kept his desires secret from his wife at first. But then he dropped hints. "I'd leave a nightgown around, and she was displeased.

"I hadn't realized how dysfunctional [that first wife] was," Dawn Marie tells me. "Not just sexually, but how she didn't take care of the house. She wouldn't support me at all except sometimes she'd give in and I'd wear a bra and nightgown to bed. The bra was the most important thing. I've been seeing a therapist, who told me I wear the bra and fake breasts because they're a replacement for my lost mother."

This is what I am hearing: a man climbs into bed in a slithery nightie and a bra stuffed with nylons, and calls his wife "dysfunctional" for not being happy about it. As for Dawn Marie's second wife, to whom he was married for nearly thirteen years, Dawn Marie has this to say: "She was a really ugly, miserable, terrible person." Dawn Marie married her because she was beautiful on the outside, a lapse Dawn Marie concedes was a big mistake. To this woman, Dawn Marie's proclivities were a colossal turn-off. If she really loved him, he suggested, she would have embraced his feminine side.

Since her paid leave from a major corporation began, Dawn Marie has busied herself with charitable work and digital photography. I ask if she's on any hormones. "Oh no," she says. "I've never even thought about that." She—he—is, first, a man, with all the accompanying urges. For years he attended singles dances, until a mutual friend introduced him to the woman he calls his fiancée.

Dawn Marie told her about the cross-dressing when they'd been dating three weeks. "Those first weeks were fabulous," she says of the time before she revealed her secret obsession. "I'd invite her over for dinners. I'd do all the cooking, and I'm very fastidious about the presentation—each meal is like a work of art." The fiancée, who's three years older than Dawn Marie, couldn't help noticing "little things about the way I kept my house—the satin sheets, the feminine colors. When we went shopping I knew more about female fashion than she did."

Is this possible? As Dawn Marie keeps up his immodest patter it occurs to me that this fiancée was in for two surprises. First, her boyfriend sometimes preferred to be a girl; second, he was damn good at it—better, in some ways, than she was. "She was amazed what I knew about femininity," Dawn Marie says. "I invited her over one evening and said I needed to speak with her. She already knew I wasn't the normal macho guy. I told her there are people in this world who for some reason have female tendencies. I told her I had lots of lingerie around the house and I was planning to go to Fantasia Fair. I said, I don't want to get into a relationship without being honest."

The girlfriend responded that she'd need time to get comfortable with the news. However, Dawn Marie knew she was already hooked. "I was very attentive sexually," she tells me. "I knew what she needed—the softness, the foreplay."

Like Bonnie, Dawn Marie dismisses his fiancée's initial reluctance to fully embrace his female fantasies. She jokes about how the fiancée got through her first Fantasia Fair with the help of Valium. "She was having problems at first." But ultimately, Dawn Marie says, the fiancée had to agree she'd never met a nicer group of people. "And now when we come here we don't have to be tied at the hip," she says. "She can meet with the other girls. I'm one of the most fortunate men here."

And then, to change the subject, Dawn Marie blurts, "But we haven't really talked about breasts! I have the most realistic breast forms. They warm to the touch." She buys the forms at Glamour Boutiques in Auburn, Massachusetts. They usually sell for about $175 a pair but the store gives her a deal because she shops there "in very large volume." These high-end breast forms are silicone and lifelike with a heavy "skin," anatomically correct nipples, and areolas, she tells me. "I just replaced my set this year."

I'd love to see one. Dawn Marie promptly obliges. But she does not, as one might expect, reach under the stretchy ballet neckline of her dress to pluck one out. (I later polled my women friends, all of whom said they would have retrieved the breast in this way.) What Dawn Marie does is bend down, grab the dress's hem with both hands, and lift the dress up over her head to reveal, well, everything. There before me is the whole enchilada. Nude pantyhose hold firmly in place a "gaff," panties designed to compress the male genitalia. Rising from the pantyhose is an impressively taut belly; hovering above that, a white Calvin Klein bra, from which Dawn Marie extracts something looking eerily indistinguishable from a human breast. She places the thing in my outstretched hand where it lies, warm, fleshy, and crowned by an erect nipple wreathed in a plum areola. I test its weight as if buying a Cornish hen, but I am momentarily speechless.

"It's um, great!" I finally manage to say. Dawn Marie is visibly cheered and eager to offer the specs. "I'm wearing a thin bra so you can see the nipple," she explains. "The bra is size 36C but the breasts are what they call a full B. I prefer the full B because I wear these all the time—I sleep in them at night—and the C breast forms have an annoying tendency to peek out under clothes. They'd still look natural, but the B stays completely in the cup."

I hand Dawn Marie the warm breast, but before I do I get this really infantile urge to say, "I'm not giving it back: ha ha ha!" and make her chase me around the room in her pumps. Something about the circumstances makes me want to misbehave.

"I can't tell you how many bras I've been through," she says. "Tell me about it," I reply. "I have an account with Victoria's Secret," Dawn Marie adds, "so I ordered that IPEX bra and I couldn't get my breasts in! I think it's designed so your nipples won't show. There's thicker padding toward the nipple, but I don't see why you'd want to cover up the nipples.

"I *love* breasts," Dawn Marie continues. "I realize females come in every size and shape and I enjoy female breasts immensely. But I've been out with women who pass the pencil test and aren't responsive at all, and others who, the minute you go near them, they're your slave." Interestingly put. I wonder what I'll do if she asks to see mine. "What bothers me is when women wear bras that show seams and quilting," she says. "You know, the kind where you don't see the breast form."

Apparently Dawn Marie's expertise in bras and breast forms was not lost on his fiancée. According to Dawn Marie, the poor woman didn't have't a clue. "I told her to go get a fitting," she says. "I introduced her to high-end bras, like Bali." Like *Bali*? I hate to sound like a snob, but referring to Bali as "high-end" is like going to Applebee's for haute cuisine. I keep my mouth shut. Who am I, the expert? "There are so many things my fiancée has acquired from me," Dawn Marie says "She's wearing Bali bras now after borrowing mine. I also enjoy the Body by Victoria line. Now guess who's wearing it! And we use the same perfume—I used it first. It's called Angel. Before we came here, I had to reclaim my earrings, my skirts . . . There are times when we go out and she's wearing my bra brand and my earrings."

There is a short silence, during which Dawn Marie is sizing me up. "Now would you mind if I ask you a few questions?" Ask away, I say. "Do you have a partner, a man or a woman?" she asks. "I have a husband," I reply. "Does he ask you to dress up—you know, in stockings, garter belt, that sort of thing?" "Nope." Dawn Marie is stunned. "Well how about lingerie?" I confess to Dawn Marie that my husband refers to my sleepwear as "Frederick's of Anchorage." Dawn Marie says this is a lost opportunity indeed. She looks me up and down. "My fiancée has a body like yours."

Dawn Marie says she can't speak for other cross-dressers but that during Fantasia Fair she'll be wearing the breast forms "twenty-four/seven." "It's not a sexual arousal thing, but it's a comfort thing," she explains. "Their bounce, their feel, it brings an inner peace. I'm not into flaunting them, or I'd have DDs."

Sometimes at home Dawn Marie and her fiancée play as girlfriends. When Dawn Marie is planning to dress, her fiancée likes to lay out her bra and breast forms, a small but tender gesture that bowls her over every time. "If I could wear these breast forms and this bra all the time, I'd be very happy. When I lie in bed, I'll fall asleep with the nipple in the palm of my hand, cupping the breast. It doesn't matter anymore that they're not connected because I almost feel that way."

Then, flashing a warm, knowing gaze, Dawn Marie says: "I imagine I feel exactly the same way you do."

My encounter with Dawn Marie left me wondering: Could it be true? Could a man come to know and identify with me more deeply by walking a mile, so to speak, in my bra? But my breasts—all women's breasts—amount to so much more than traffic stoppers and marital aids. I have never nursed a child, but unlike Dawn Marie's state-of-the-art prosthetic boobs and Bonnie's sturdy silicone implants, my breasts were designed to nourish and nurture. Part of me will always relate to them that way. Expendable as they might be, women's breasts are inextricably woven into the mystery of what it is to be and feel feminine. I don't fault Dawn Marie for sleeping blissfully while cradling her chemically self-warming breast forms. But it takes far more than boobs and a flowing nightgown to feel the way real women feel, living in these bodies as we grow, blossom, and age.

Epilogue:
What I Learned at the Front

T HE MEN I'VE spoken to confess an almost hypnotic obsession with breasts. One described sitting in a café near a woman he'd never met. He didn't find the woman particularly attractive, but he took note of her huge boobs. He returned to his morning paper until he saw the woman spill coffee on her blouse, immediately wet a napkin, and begin to work the spreading stain just above her nipple. Up and down she rubbed, seemingly oblivious to her surroundings.

My friend was excited and transfixed. In his temporarily demented state, he wondered whether he was being teased. "I was thinking, This isn't fair—you're killing me here!" he recalled.

We are talking about a woman haplessly swabbing coffee off herself, not a stripper twirling her tassels. My friend is not proud of the ease with which a pair of female orbs throws off his ability to focus on the task at hand. A sane, thoughtful human being with consequential things on his mind, at the sight of large breasts he goes uncontrollably gaga. Like him, other men sheepishly admit that big boobs can transform them into the biggest boobs in the room.

These same men, when making tender love to their wives or girlfriends, are likely to kiss, fondle, and lick their partners' breasts, whatever they look like, with a kind of reverence. The same construction worker who crudely hollers, "Nice tits!" goes home to gently cup the breasts of his wife, or watch in affectionate amazement as she takes their baby to her nipple.

As for women, we seem to be no less breast-obsessed, though in a different way. Millions pine for larger breasts, while many long for breasts that are less cumbersome and more petite. There seems to be no end to the ways in which women are willing to make this happen, whether it's going under the scalpel, sleeping in an unwieldy suction gizmo, or getting smacked hard on the back. Otherwise well-adjusted women hand over their earnings and take leave of their senses for the elusive promise of gaining one cup size. Though we are free to guzzle Bustea or chomp on Bust-Up gum all day, nothing really works except surgery, which carries serious risks and costs more than many can reasonably afford.

And for what? Increasingly, women who long for bigger breasts are taking their cue from anorexic, saline-stuffed models and movie stars. Huge breasts on an otherwise lithe frame is an ideal practically no woman comes by naturally. Since breasts are essentially sacks of fat, it is highly unlike that a ninety-pound waif will be hauling real boobs weighing a few pounds each. Is this body type really even attractive? The mainstream media seduce us—well, more like pummel us—into thinking this is the body of every man's dreams. Though it's a body you'll rarely see on a friend, neighbor, or gym acquaintance, it's precisely this body, with boobs out to here, that is employed to sell us everything from cars to shampoo to boobs themselves.

It takes time for young women to befriend and grow comfortable with their breasts. I remember those years of painful self-consciousness, when I felt as if my boobs were on their way to taking over the rest of me, like a form of kudzu. But with age comes perspective; after all, we are talking about two "stupid mounds of flesh," as Dr. Khouri would put it. So I was intrigued to find that many male and female transvestites and transsexuals see breasts as the essential emblem of femininity. For men like Dawn Marie, a pair of breasts, even ones you can play catch with, confers womanhood all by itself. To the obvious question, Why are men the world over endlessly obsessed with boobs, especially big ones?, I found no single answer. I'll leave the evolutionary theorists to continue pondering.

But it's no mystery that breasts can be a lot of fun for both Dick and Jane. Breasts feel good. They are soft and yummy to the touch, and having a lover pay serious attention to them is one of life's great sensual pleasures. Long after they're weaned, children know exactly where to nuzzle for maximum warmth and comfort. And despite guys' fascination with porn and the bodacious Barbie-babe who taunts us from every billboard and TV screen, ultimately men seem as content as babies are with the breasts, large or small, to which they've been granted free and familiar access.

As for my own DDDs, in middle age I have come to accept, embrace, and even adore them. They're in pretty good shape. I've learned how to carry them comfortably, even if that means encasing them in bras that cost more than a flight to Bermuda. They suit me now more than ever, at a time in my life when I feel confident and sexy but don't take myself—or them—too seriously. I have grown accustomed to, and almost fatalistic about the unceasing stares and comments they still attract, and, okay, I admit it, I may even experience a pang of loss if and when those stares cease.

That said, I always have and always will want to be appreciated first and foremost as the person I am on the inside. A person who happens to be stacked.

Acknowledgments

For their generous advice and encouragement I'd like to thank my editors Karen Rinaldi, Amanda Katz, and Michael O'Connor; my agent, Susan Ramer; Joe Ryan; Howie Schneider; and my best friend, Sophia Schneider.